A Practical Guide to Teaching History in the Secondary School

Edited by Martin Hunt

Routledge
Taylor & Francis Group

LONDON AND NEW YORK

First published 2007 by Routledge
2 Park Square, Milton Park, Abingdon, Oxon OX14 4RN

Simultaneously published in the USA and Canada
by Routledge
270 Madison Ave, New York, NY10016

Routledge is an imprint of the Taylor & Francis Group, an informa business

© 2007 Martin Hunt, selection and editorial matter; individual chapters,
the contributors.

Typeset in Palatino by Keystroke, 28 High Street, Tettenhall, Wolverhampton
Printed and bound in Great Britain by Bell & Bain Ltd, Glasgow

British Library Cataloguing in Publication Data
A catalogue record for this book is available from the British Library

Library of Congress Cataloging in Publication Data
A catalog record for this book has been requested

ISBN 10: 0–415–37024–8 (pbk)
ISBN 10: 0–203–02983–6 (ebk)

ISBN 13: 978–0–415–37024–0 (pbk)
ISBN 13: 978–0–203–02983–1 (ebk)

A Practical Guide to Teaching History in the Secondary School

A Practical Guide to Teaching History in the Secondary School provides practical guidance, ideas and tasks to support trainee history teachers and their mentors. It will also help the development of imaginative lessons on aspects of history teaching in a variety of different content areas and teaching situations. Newly qualified and beginning teachers should also find it useful.

This accessible workbook includes a range of features, designed to improve practical teaching skills, particularly in those areas of acknowledged concern and difficulty for the trainee history teacher. These features include:

- case studies
- examples of existing good practice
- a range of tried-and-tested strategies
- examples of the use of ICT

Also provided is a wealth of helpful resources and training materials. Activities in each chapter provide a toolkit to help trainee history teachers analyse their learning and performance. The book has been designed to be written in directly, and so provide a useful record.

This book complements and extends the best-selling textbook, *Learning to Teach History in the Secondary School* (also published by Routledge), providing detailed examples of theory in practice. The authors use their extensive experience of working in schools and with trainee history teachers to analyse and explain successful teaching approaches and show how current issues and debates influence decision making.

In addition, this book has a companion website which provides further guidance, more exemplar material and links to further reading. This workbook will be invaluable to all trainee history teachers.

Martin Hunt was a Principal Lecturer and PGCE Secondary Course Leader at Manchester Metropolitan University, UK.

Routledge Teaching Guides

Series Editors: Susan Capel and Marilyn Leask

Other titles in the series:

A Practical Guide to Teaching Physical Education in the Secondary School
Edited by Susan Capel, Peter Breckon and Jean O'Neill

A Practical Guide to Teaching Modern Foreign Languages in the Secondary School
Edited by Norbert Pachler and Ana Redondo

A Practical Guide to Teaching Citizenship in the Secondary School
Edited by Liam Gearon

A Practical Guide to Teaching ICT in the Secondary School
Edited by Steve Kennewell

These Practical Guides have been designed as companions to **Learning to Teach (subject) in the Secondary School**. For further information on the Routledge Teaching Guides series please visit our website at www.routledge.com/education

Contents

Series Editors' Introduction

This practical and accessible workbook is part of a series of textbooks for student teachers. It complements and extends the popular textbook entitled *Learning to Teach in the Secondary School: A Companion to School Experience*, as well as the subject-specific textbook *Learning to Teach History in the Secondary School*. We anticipate that you will want to use this book in conjunction with these other books.

Teaching is rapidly becoming a more research- and evidence-informed profession. We have used research and professional evidence about what makes good practice to underpin the 'Learning to Teach in the Secondary School' series and these practical workbooks. Both the generic and subject-specific book in the series provide theoretical, research and professional evidence-based advice and guidance to support you as you focus on developing aspects of your teaching or your pupils' learning as you progress through your initial teacher education course and beyond.

This book aims to reinforce your understanding of aspects of your teaching, support you in aspects of your development as a teacher and your teaching and enable you to analyse your success as a teacher in maximising pupils' learning by focusing on practical applications. The practical activities in this book can be used in a number of ways. Some activities are designed to be undertaken by you individually, others as a joint task in pairs and yet others as group work working with, for example, other student teachers or a school- or university-based tutor. Your tutor may use the activities with a group of student teachers. The book has been designed so that you can write directly into it.

In England, new ways of working for teachers are being developed through an initiative remodelling the school workforce. This may mean that you have a range of colleagues to support in your classroom. They also provide an additional resource on which you can draw. In any case, you will, of course, need to draw on additional resources to support your development and the *Learning to Teach in the Secondary School, 4th edition* website (http://www.routledge.com/textbooks/0415363926) lists key websites for Scotland, Wales, Northern Ireland and England. For example, key websites relevant to teachers in England include the Teacher Training Resource Bank (www.ttrb.ac.uk). Others include: www.teachernet.gov.uk which is part of the DfES schools web initiative; www.becta.org.uk, which has ICT resources; and www.qca.org.uk which is the Qualifications and Curriculum Authority website.

We do hope that this practical workbook will be useful in supporting your development as a teacher.

Susan Capel
Marilyn Leask
May 2006

List of illustrations

FIGURES

TABLES

Contributors

Christopher Chambers is a Senior Lecturer in Education at Manchester Metropolitan University, teaching PGCE trainees. He was previously Head of Humanities at Prestwich High School, Bury.

Ian Dicksee was Head of History and Quality Manager at Henbury High School, Macclesfield, and professional and subject mentor for Manchester Metropolitan University, before taking up his teaching post in Cyprus.

Simon Goodwin is Head of Humanities at Great Sankey High School, Warrington with 12 years' experience as a subject mentor for Manchester Metropolitan University.

Steve Guscott is Head of History and Citizenship at St James' Catholic Humanities College, Cheadle Hulme, Stockport.

Martin Hunt was a Principal Lecturer in Education and PGCE Secondary Course Leader at Manchester Metropolitan University.

Yvonne Sinclair is a Senior Lecturer in Education at Manchester Metropolitan University, teaching PGCE trainees, and having previously taught in schools in Oldham.

Bill Smith teaches history at Westhoughton High School, Bolton. He was a lecturer in medieval history at the Universities of Manchester and Sheffield. He is lead teacher in history for Bolton LEA.

Alison Stephen is Head of History at Abraham Moss High School, Manchester, a school where 60 per cent of its pupils have EAL with 59 languages spoken. She previously taught history in Budapest, a grammar school and a comprehensive school. She also contributes to the PGCE course at Manchester Metropolitan University.

Gail Wake was an AST and history teacher at Buile Hill High School, Salford, working with history departments across the LEA to promote quality history teaching. She is now KS3 co-ordinator in History at St. Mary's Catholic H. S, Wigan.

Acknowledgements

The editor would like to acknowledge with thanks the additional contributions of Christopher Chambers, Simon Goodwin, Ryder Hargreaves, Terry Haydn, Yvonne Sinclair, Alison Stephen and Lisa Whitby to this book.

Chapter 1   Introduction

MARTIN HUNT

In learning to teach history, the trainee teacher will experience a range of concerns, which change over the course of the training year; some are general to trainees of all subjects, others are specifically related to history and will differ from one person to another. This book attempts to offer guidance towards meeting the subject-specific concerns that surface during the course of the year. Also important is the work of practising teachers who also have experience of working as mentors with trainees.

A book of this size has to be selective and no attempt has been made to cover several important areas such as post-16 teaching. The focus is rather on those years of the secondary school likely to involve the trainees for most of their time and the subject-specific challenges they are likely to face. To a degree, the sequence of chapters follows that of *Learning to Teach History in the Secondary School*, 2nd edn (also published by Routledge). However, this book confines itself to the practical dimension with an emphasis on activities for the trainee while offering practical advice. While all chapters could be of use to trainees at any time, it is intended that the first three chapters concentrate more on the concerns of the early stages of the training year, while the rest offer guidance for that time when the trainees feel more comfortable in the classroom. Thus the chapters range from the beginner's concerns with exposition and presenting a historical narrative, teaching content that they always thought uninspiring, identifying appropriate objectives, questioning, setting purposeful tasks and group work to the more sophisticated challenges of planning for inclusion, differentiation, teaching a second-order concept such as causation, historical interpretations and their significance and using formative assessment, several of which continue to challenge more established teachers. A further strand of the book is an attempt to encourage the trainee to use a range of approaches within a selection from larger topics; hence concentration on role play, presentation technology and peer assessment. All chapters contain exemplar material but most curriculum materials, which support the chapters have been placed on the companion website http://www.routledge.com/textbooks/9780415370240.

While it is not intended to present 'off the shelf' lessons, such examples show the application of general principles into the everyday practice of experienced teachers. Thus the book is both a practical guide and a workbook. The activities are intended to complement exercises already offered by a course and to be used usually as part of the trainee's school-based work. They are designed to help trainees clarify their thoughts about the issues and the approaches they will meet, especially current debates and challenges of teaching history, to reflect on what is seen and done in the secondary school and to encourage experimentation. It is hoped that they will also help history subject mentors in their work with the trainees.

While most chapters present a mixture of activities, they also reflect the separate individuality of the authors with their own ideas and enthusiasms. Even so, several themes recur across the chapters, which are of significance for the trainee history teacher. These include the necessity of ensuring students possess adequate historical knowledge before moving on to consider the second-order concepts; the need for precision and clarity in the articulation of objectives and outcomes to promote a better quality of learning and the assessment of that learning. Several authors stress and illustrate the importance of starters in lessons, the use of key questions, the relationship of lessons to larger themes and, as several exemplar lessons allocate what seems a generous amount of time to a topic, the conviction that this is time well spent if historical understanding is developed.

The activities and ideas in the book are there for you to develop and apply to different content and contexts. Some will probably work at once but others will need refining. There are times when even the best-planned lesson does not meet your expectations, but do not be too hard on yourself, as some very able trainee teachers sometimes are. Think about the approach, analyse it, adjust and try again.

Good luck!

Chapter 2   Why learn history?

MARTIN HUNT

INTRODUCTION

There will be times when you feel you have to explain the value of learning history in the secondary school to a variety of people: senior staff, colleagues teaching other subjects, parents and your pupils, so it is important that you have a good grasp of the varied aims of history (see Haydn, Arthur and Hunt, 2001, *Learning to Teach History in the Secondary School*, Routledge, p. 20). However, here the concern is confined to establishing the value of learning history in the eyes of your pupils. Pupils need to know the answer to the question 'Why are we doing this?', especially if they are considering taking history beyond the age of 14 (see Biddulph and Adey, 2003). You need to have thought through those aims in such a way that they are easily understood by the pupils. Furthermore, the process of such articulation at the level of individual lessons, or a series of lessons, not only will clarify in your own mind what you are trying to achieve but will also enable you to emphasise those aims in the way in which you construct and deliver the lesson. Vagueness of purpose can lead to uninspiring lessons.

Chapter aims

By the end of the chapter you should be able to:

- select from a variety of aims for the teaching of history those which are particularly related to a specific lesson or series of lessons;
- be precise in identifying the range of key concepts, which are fundamental to the learning of history within a lesson or series of lessons;
- be able to articulate the aims of history in everyday language, accessible to most secondary school pupils;
- be able to identify the key skills, i.e. communication, number, ICT, problem solving, learning to work with others, that require further development in a lesson or series of lessons;
- show how a history lesson or series of lessons has significance, noting precisely how events and issues in the past contribute to pupils' understanding of the world in which they live.

THE VALUE OF LEARNING HISTORY

In this chapter, the focus will be on the value of learning history as it emerges from individual lessons. We begin by considering a couple of lessons on the Agricultural Revolution for a Year 8 or 9 class. This topic has been chosen as an example because in recent years there has been a tendency for trainee history teachers to view this topic as being dry and dull in the same way as the Industrial Revolution. One recent trainee wrote, in a questionnaire asking trainees to identify the challenges they had faced, of the difficulty of 'getting pupils to understand the relevance of farming in the eighteenth century to today's modern world', while admitting that his own lack of enthusiasm for the topic would not have helped. Thus there is a real challenge to trainees to realise just how relevant a topic such as the Agricultural Revolution can be to the development of the pupils' historical understanding. Without such conviction, lessons on the topic would indeed be dry and perfunctory. The contention here is that this topic offers plenty of scope for interesting and lively lessons and moreover provides good examples of why pupils should learn history. The two lessons involve the class using information to advise a fictitious farmer on how he could achieve the profits from his farm to improve his lifestyle. The two lessons used 13 PowerPoint slides and worksheets.

<table>
<tr><td>WWW</td><td>For the curriculum material associated with these lessons, see:

http://www.routledge.com/textbooks/9780415370240</td></tr>
</table>

EXEMPLAR LESSON ONE

Starter	Using the PowerPoint presentation, the class is presented with a decision-making exercise involving a tenant farmer, Jacob Newmarch, in the early eighteenth century. Slides 2, 3 and 4 describe his situation, his farming and his ambitions. The information on these slides may also be presented in a handout.
Phase 2	Slide 5 shows Jacob's balance sheet for 1725. Pupils have a copy of this on a worksheet. After the items have been explained, pupils, using calculators, work out the total costs and sales and discover the annual profit. Differentiation is achieved by giving more or less information.
Phase 3	Slide 6 moves the story on to 1730. The price of grain has fallen although costs and the yield per acre remain the same. The class work out, again with the information on the worksheet, details of the new sales and profit figures and realise Jacob faces a real threat to his ambitions, even to his livelihood.
Phase 4	Jacob has a crisis. What can he do? In groups, pupils have five minutes to work out 'a business plan' at first without using textbooks. Then, using textbooks, they look for other suggestions. Each group needs to be able to present a six-point business plan for Jacob.
Plenary	Teacher fields responses and summarises what has been covered.

EXEMPLAR LESSON TWO

Starter	Recap Jacob's problems (slide 6) and the suggested improvements summarised on slide 7.
Phase 2	Distribute second pupil worksheet. This includes a new balance sheet (slide 8), noting the increased costs but also the greatly increased yield from 12 bushels per acre to 24. (A bushel = ¼ hundredweight or 28 lbs.) Pupils calculate the new income and profit. Can Jacob now meet his ambitions?
Phase 3	Brief survey of pasture farming changes, using textbook.
Phase 4	Matters arising: developing historical understanding Using notes on their worksheets, pupils in pairs suggest reasons for the farming improvements. Give target of five reasons. Field answers (slide 9 has some, there could be others). Ask supplementary related questions. What was the most important reason? Was there one single cause that would have produced these changes? Pupils note the points on the worksheet.
Phase 5	Developing historical understanding Pupils asked to consider what the consequences of the changes were (slide 10). Question and answer to tease out five or six consequences, noting their long-term effects and thus their continuing impact. Pupils make notes.
Plenary	Developing historical understanding Show completed slide 11 (details on pupil worksheet 2). Explain each of the points in turn linked to 'why learn history?'. Set written work (slide 12).

When these lessons were given to three mixed ability Year 9 classes in an inner city comprehensive, the teacher's preparation involved the simplification of some of the language on the slides, the addition of a couple of pictures and also the creation of a final slide (no. 13), which was printed as a helpsheet for less able pupils. Additionally and crucially a set of calculators was borrowed from the mathematics department. In their response the pupils were able to say why we sometimes need to be able to use numbers in history. Both the teacher and the class said that they had found it useful to focus on the problems facing one individual and the pupils showed that they did understand the significance of the agricultural changes. The following two activities consider two issues that arise from these lessons.

Activity 2.1 Focusing on an individual

Focusing on one individual and his family helped to make the changes in agriculture more meaningful to the pupils than generalised statements. Using your school's history department syllabus or a textbook with social and economic topics, try to identify other content areas, usually *involving changing circumstances*, which could similarly benefit from a focus on an individual family. In each case, consider how this approach would help you to explain the reasons for studying the topic.

Activity 2.2   Use of numeracy

In *Numeracy across the Curriculum* (DfEE, 2001), the DfEE has been encouraging subjects across the secondary curriculum to reinforce pupils' numeracy skills, e.g. Arithmetic, graphs and charts. Numeracy can play a part as a useful tool in the provision of stimulating history lessons and often can be used to draw out the significance of an event.

1   Consider in turn how the following National Curriculum topics could include such skills often through developing pupils' understanding of the economic factors that affect people in different classes of society and the impact of economic and technological developments on people at different times in the past: (i) nineteenth-century working and living conditions; (ii) decline of the handloom weavers; (iii) disease in the industrial town; (iv) factory and coal owners' profits.

2   Read Ian Phillips (2002), 'History : Mathematics or History with Mathematics: does it add up?' How does he show the way the use of numeracy in history can be used to emphasise the significance of an event as well as the importance of studying the topic? See also Davies *et al.* (2003), *Enlivening Secondary History: 40 Classroom Activities for Teachers and Pupils*, also published by Routledge, for a set of activities using numeracy, as well as other examples on the website.

After reading the details about the two lessons and the information on the PowerPoint slides, you are now in a position to attempt three associated activities.

RELATING AIMS TO SPECIFIC LESSONS

In the past 30 or more years many lists of school aims have appeared and over these years different emphases have been given to those aims. At times they have been subject to lengthy and sometimes acrimonious debate (see *Learning to Teach History in the Secondary School*, 2nd edn, Routledge, Chapter 2, for more on this debate). This book places emphasis on the more practical application of these aims.

Activity 2.3 includes one of the lists of aims, the nine purposes of school history produced by the History Working Group in 1988 in anticipation of the National Curriculum. These are all worthy aims and some teachers will rate some more highly than others. Yet for you as a trainee teacher, their generality could limit their value. It is therefore a useful exercise to go through each one in turn and to ask 'What does this really mean in terms of the lessons I give to 9Y?' Certainly, the language of the general aims is not what you could use to answer a pupil asking the question, 'Why learn history?' And yet in order to have that precision of intent and conviction of value so necessary for a successful teacher, you need to be able to unpack these aims so they are more precise and can be expressed in everyday language accessible to most secondary students.

The second and third parts of this activity make use of the lessons on the Agricultural Revolution. The aim of these exercises is to help you to make the connections between these general aims and specific lessons. Hopefully you will find the lessons can connect to more of the aims than you might have first realised and that in turn enhances your appreciation of what you are teaching and why it is important to learn history.

Activity 2.3 Relating aims to specific lessons

Nine purposes of school history

1   To help understand the present in the context of the past.
2   To arouse interest in the past.
3   To help to give pupils a sense of identity.
4   To help give pupils an understanding of their own cultural roots and shared inheritance.
5   To contribute to the pupils' knowledge and understanding of other countries and other cultures in the modern world.
6   To train the mind by means of disciplined study.
7   To introduce pupils to the distinctive methodology of historians.
8   To encourage other areas of the curriculum.
9   To prepare pupils for adult life.

(History Working Group 1988)

1   Go through each of the nine purposes in turn and try to work out what these aims could mean in precise terms and in words, which are accessible to the majority of secondary school pupils.
2   Using the above list of aims, select those which you think are applicable to the two Agricultural Revolution lessons, noting at which place that aim is being addressed.

_____

_____

3   Are there any other aims, not on this list, which you think show the importance of learning history?

_____

_____

_____

CATEGORISING OUTCOMES

The aim of Activity 2.4 is to develop your ability to identify and to categorise the various learning outcomes that can result from history lessons. You are asked to proceed through each of the phases of the two lessons on the Agricultural Revolution and to decide how that phase contributes to specific learning outcomes. For this task the outcomes are divided into three main areas – knowledge, key concepts and key skills – but you need to be precise about what knowledge, which key concepts and which key skills are being addressed by that phase.

These three areas of knowledge, concepts and skills may be said to be at the heart of why we learn history; all are important and debates about the pre-eminence of one area over another obscure the reality of their interrelatedness. Before you begin to complete Activity 2.4, it may be helpful to make a few comments about these three areas.

7

Activity 2.4   Categorising outcomes

1   Identify the specific learning outcomes that arise from each phase.

Lesson One	Knowledge	Key Concepts	Key Skills
Phase 1			
2			
3			
4			
5			

Lesson Two	Knowledge	Key Concepts	Key Skills
Phase 2			
3			
4 (i)			
4 (ii)			
4 (iii)			

2   Try to identify what is unique about these two lessons that would not be covered by any other subject in the National Curriculum.

Activity 2.3 *continued*

3   Write an explanation in no more than 100 words of what the pupils are gaining from these two lessons in language that you think would be accessible to the majority of secondary school pupils.

_____

_____

_____

_____

_____

_____

_____

_____

_____

_____

_____

_____

_____

_____

Knowledge

Consider the range of knowledge covered. This includes not just the broad terms such as the open field system but also new words such as Land Tax, bushel and fallow, and possibly new substantive concepts, in this case, many economic ones, such as profit, income, investment. It is important that you are aware of what new knowledge your pupils are to acquire in advance so that you will not make assumptions and will have thought through your explanation. In considering the nature of subject knowledge it is also useful if you have become familiar with the areas of knowledge and understanding related to subject knowledge as specified in the Revised Standards (http://tda.gov.uk/teachers/professional standards.aspx).

Key concepts

For the completion of this column of Activity 2.4, you will need to consider what are the key concepts in the learning of history (see *Learning to Teach History in the Secondary School*, 2nd edn, Routledge, Chapters 5 and 6, where these are discussed comprehensively). For the purposes of this exercise you will be looking to see how each phase can contribute to extending pupils' historical understanding about time and chronology, about the characteristic features of the past, cause and consequence, change and continuity, interpretations, evidence and historical significance.

Key skills

A more recent development in the changing curriculum has been the stipulation that all subjects should contribute to the development of 'key skills'. These include communication, number, ICT, problem solving, 'learning to learn' and 'learning to work with others'.

One further area *not* covered by the activity concerns the contribution the learning of history could make to the spiritual, moral, social and cultural development of the pupils. However, the two lessons on the Agricultural Revolution could raise interesting questions such as 'Has Jacob Newmarch enhanced the quality of life not just for himself but also for his community? Was there more than self-interest involved?'

LINKING A TOPIC TO OUTCOMES

Activity 2.5 helps you to link a topic to learning outcomes for the pupils. The example of the abolition of the slave trade, while showing the range of such outcomes, includes further social and moral issues.

Activity 2.5 Linking a topic to outcomes

Study Figure 2.1, which shows a range of outcomes for the pupil, which could ensue from the study of the slave trade and its abolition.

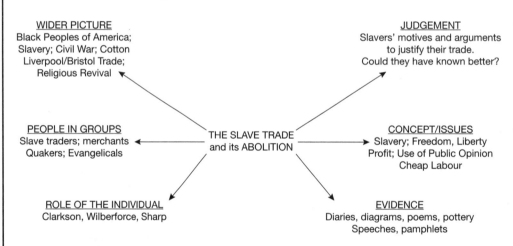

Figure 2.1 The slave trade and its abolition

1   Take a topic, which you will be teaching and try to construct a similar diagram based on that topic.
2   How could you adapt the diagram you have constructed to indicate to the pupils why they have studied that topic?
3   How could you use the information from your diagram to explain to an adult (parent, governor, headteacher) the value of studying such a topic?

DISTINGUISHING BETWEEN CONSEQUENCES AND SIGNIFICANCE

Activity 2.6 highlights the importance of emphasising the value of each individual topic that is studied. The message is that, having made pupils aware of the principal details of a topic, *this is not the time to move on to the next topic*, but the time to reinforce the learning by concentrating the pupils' minds on those key concepts, which are related to the topic. Always remember the 'matters arising'! In this regard, such applications as reasons for change, most important cause, choice of one single cause that would have brought about change are well established. Less so are those of consequence and significance and yet in considering the question 'Why learn history?', these have a vital part to play. They are challenging to teach, but every effort should be made to develop them (see *Learning to Teach History in the Secondary School*, 2nd edn, Routledge, pp. 26–7, 119–23). Having taught the Agricultural Revolution lessons, the teacher was to return to the topic after the study of the Industrial Revolution to help reinforce pupils' overview of the topic, to help them to see the big picture, showing a topic can have significance for times other than today. In completing the exercise you may not always agree with the inclusion of some of the statements and may have better alternatives. You may also find that the distinction between consequence and significance is not always clear and this may prompt useful discussion with tutors, mentors and fellow trainees.

Activity 2.6 Distinguishing between consequences and significance

1   Tick the appropriate column to indicate whether the statements below describe the consequences of changes in agriculture *or* the significance of those changes.

Statement	Consequence	Significance
Increased food production		
Helped Britain to become the first major industrial nation		
Improved the nation's health		
Shows the value of investment to reap, literally, a reward		
Shows the value of encouraging invention and preparedness for change		
More people were available for non-farming work, e.g. industry		
Showed that wealth creation in one area leads to better employment all round		
Revived the rural economy not just for farmers but others such as blacksmiths and millers		
Showed the value of spreading new ideas		
Changed the landscape with hedges, fences, walls, farmhouses built away from the village		
Showed how changes occur because of the variety of pressures, e.g. personal ambition, invention, economic necessity.		

Activity 2.6 *continued*

2 Enter your choices of 'significance' in the left-hand column and then try to think of present-day examples of the same statement.

Significance of the study of the Agricultural Revolution for the present day	Present-day Examples

The aim of the second exercise in this activity is to encourage you to continue to think about that relationship between the historical topic being studied and the present. Thus, in the case of the exemplar lessons, it is important for pupils to develop further their understanding of current developments such as the impact of new inventions and technology on local employment and communities and how people responded to those changes.

LINKING PAST AND PRESENT

This final activity pursues further the linking of past and present as an aid to answering the question, 'Why learn history?'

Activity 2.7 Linking past and present

High on the list of aims for the teaching and learning of history is the claim that the subject helps students to understand the present from the study of the past. It is always useful to be able to link the topics you teach to the present. It need not be an ephemeral exercise as, often sadly, the same topics recur and can be built into your planning of starters and plenaries.

1   Using television Ceefax or Teletext select a series of items over a few days and (a) work out the wider issue, the bigger picture to which it belongs, and (b) work out the historical links and themes. Three are completed below as examples.

News item	Wider issues	Historical links
A&E Depts. warned over care	*Role of the state; NHS; private medicine. Costs of provision*	*Provision of care for the ill and injured in earlier times; development of hospitals; growth of the welfare state*
Race to save 102 Chinese miners in flooded mine	*Use of energy resources; Dangers of mining*	*Dangers of mining – water, gas etc., Mines Act 1842; Child and female labour; Changing sources of energy*
Space shuttle return held up 24 hours	*Technological advances; pioneering, exploration*	*Impact of technological change; dangers to explorers; achievements of pioneers*

2   Discuss with your mentor the potential value of compiling a file of newspaper articles.

Strategies for emphasising the purpose of studying a topic include:

1   Placing the topic in the wider context, e.g. the effect of technical change on the livelihood of individual and communities.
2   Identifying the learning of new words, new ideas, concepts and their use today.
3   Giving imaginative written work, e.g. Jacob Newmarch writes an article for *Annals of Agriculture* encouraging others to do what he did.
4   Re-visiting. Returning to the topic after later ones have been covered, using diagrams and possibly a concept map to show the bigger picture.

SUMMARY

This chapter has considered the question 'Why learn history?' and some of the reasons have arisen from the exemplar lessons, but not all. Little reference has been made to two aspects, use of evidence and interpretations, which are very important in answering that question. These are covered later in the book. You will find particularly in the early stages of your training that you are very preoccupied with the knowledge aspect of your teaching but do not let this distract you from the need to be aware of that tripartite combination of knowledge, concepts and skills. Due attention to the last two could well encourage a more imaginative approach to your lessons, while total concentration on knowledge could produce the opposite. You should note the value of taking the opportunity, where appropriate, of explaining why the pupils are learning a particular topic and be prepared to do so in a way the pupils will understand. Finally, you might consider the value of including in your lesson plans the identification of the significance of the topic being studied at least to yourself, showing how it can relate to events and issues in today's world.

ACKNOWLEDGEMENT

My thanks go to Alison Stephen for teaching the lessons on the agricultural changes at Abraham Moss High School, Manchester.

FURTHER READING

Counsell, C. (2004) 'Looking through a Josephine Butler shaped window: focusing pupils' thinking on historical significance', *Teaching History* 114.

Evans, R.J. (1997) *In Defence of History*, London: Granta Books.

Hunt, M. (2000) 'Teaching historical significance', Chapter 4 in J. Arthur and R. Phillips (eds) *Issues in History Teaching*, London: Routledge.

Husbands, C. (1996) *What Is History Teaching? Language, Ideas and Meaning in Learning about the Past*, Buckingham: Open University Press.

Chapter 3   Planning

GAIL WAKE AND MARTIN HUNT

INTRODUCTION

It would be an exaggeration to claim that the various challenges trainee teachers experience in the classroom can all be attributed to inadequate planning. Situations are more complex than that. However, it is possible to argue that many difficulties can be eliminated or substantially reduced by good planning. Trainee teachers will be mostly concerned with short-term planning, particularly in the early stages of a course, and then the medium-term planning as the course progresses to placement in another school. In the later stages it is more likely you will be given greater freedom to use your initiative in the planning of your lessons. The aim of this chapter is to offer some guidance for both short- and medium-term planning with associated activities, which you could use to help you with this planning.

The experiences of tutors, mentors and indeed HMI have shown that a recurrent and prevailing problem is the difficulty some trainees have in 'thinking through' their lesson planning from the initial statement of an objective or outcome right through to the confirmation that all, or most, of the students have achieved the intended outcome. At their worst, lesson plans have one, vague statement of content or objectives, which have little connection with the rest of the lesson or with what actually takes place. The challenge is fourfold. It involves:

1   the formulation of precise objectives;
2   the linking of an objective or outcome to specific phases and tasks within the lesson or tracking an objective;
3   the assessment of whether an objective or outcome has been achieved;
4   the planning either to remedy any limited achievement or to reinforce the learning that has taken place.

Chapter aims

By the end of this chapter you should be able to:

- formulate precise lesson objectives;
- ensure that your lesson objectives are clearly linked to specific phases and tasks within the lesson;
- plan the ways by which you can determine whether your objectives have been achieved;

- understand how to plan and develop resources for a unit of interrelated lessons, which includes overarching skills and understanding, has a variety of approaches and the assessment of progress;
- devise ways of evaluating your planning.

SHORT-TERM PLANNING

There are many factors involved in successful planning and many issues to consider. The breadth of these is well documented in Chapter 3 of *Learning to Teach History in the Secondary School*, 2nd edn, Routledge, 2001. Here we seek to emphasise the importance of precise thinking in your lesson planning, the ability to think through a lesson.

You have been given a topic to teach to a class. Having researched the topic, checked how it is treated in available textbooks and available resources, the ability range of the class, the first challenge you have to meet is working out the objectives or the intended outcomes of your lesson. As you begin this, you need to have some rough preliminary ideas about the phases of the lesson, your role, what the students will be doing and what resources you are likely to use and/or to create.

Selecting and formulating objectives

The key word is again 'precision'. Problems can occur when this is missing. For example, a phrase such as 'to look at a picture' is not very helpful. It does not indicate why pupils are looking at the picture and is certainly too vague to present any opportunity for assessing either understanding or skill. Even statements such as 'to develop source skills' are too vague. It can be argued that useful objectives can be built into a basic model of four blocks or phrases (Figure 3.1).

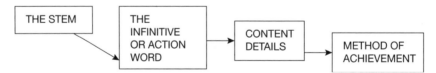

Figure 3.1 Four block model of objectives

Activity 3.1 helps you to identify your lesson objectives.

Activity 3.1 Identifying objectives

In the early days of your placement, before you observe a lesson, ask the history teacher to write down the objectives of the lesson but not show them to you. While observing the lesson and using the guidance which follows, try to work out what you think are the objectives of the lesson. After the lesson, compare and discuss the two lists.

The stem

The stem refers to the group of words you can use to begin every statement of objective. If you are producing duplicated lesson plan proformas, these can be built in to reduce the time you spend on lesson planning. Usual items are:

> To enable the pupils to . . .
> At the end of the lesson the students should be able to . . .

Such stems ensure your focus is on your expectations of the pupils and should prevent a mixture of objectives for the teacher as well as those for the pupils. Though important, it is better to keep separate the objectives for your own learning and achievement.

The infinitive or action words

These words are crucial to your precise thinking. Avoid statements such as 'to be aware of'. Some will be less tangible than others because of their limited means of assessment, e.g. a class recalling events by giving oral answers or those that relate to developing understanding of attitudes and values over a period of time, which again are not easy to assess. Even so, there is a wide selection of infinitives available to you and accurate selection will clarify what you may be trying to do in any given phase of a lesson.

Activity 3.2 encourages you to assess the utility or otherwise of a range of action words, which in turn should help you to think through the whole of your lesson plan. Vague words could lead to indecision in the classroom.

Activity 3.2 Choosing action words

Precision in lesson planning can be a challenge for the trainee teacher especially in the early stages of a course. Vagueness can lead to ill-conceived lessons and often that is associated with not thinking through the specific activities you are asking of the pupils, hence the importance of action words. Get these right and that usually helps you to work out the pupil activities. Below is a list of 24 verbs, stating what the lesson should enable the pupils to do. Some are very much more useful than others in formulating helpful objectives. Try to identify those which you think are too vague and would not easily enable you to assess their success.

Underline	Evaluate
Identify	Notice
Study	Read
Digest	Examine
Discuss	Compare
Understand	Ponder
Watch	Analyse
Sort	Recall
Consider	Write
Choose	Show
Draw	Measure
Listen	Know

Content details

'Content' here means 'material to be taught'. This could be historical information, e.g. 'the main phases of the French Revolution' or historical understanding, e.g. 'the background of the author of an interpretation', or a precise skill, e.g. 'the sufficiency of a source for the study of a topic'. Content could also describe practical skills such as drawing a time-line or making a summary within a specified word limit.

Method of achievement

This fourth block in the model describes the means by which the objective or outcome is to be achieved, as for example in 'by creating a time-chart'. This emphasises the importance of selecting methods or learning experiences, which are appropriate for the other three parts of the basic model.

How many objectives?

Given the wide variety of objectives available for selection, how many would you need for a lesson? This will vary according to the ability of the class, the length of the lesson and how selective you are about what you want to emphasise. As a general principle, you may find it practicable to restrict the number to about five or six objectives for a lesson lasting an hour to 70 minutes. These are likely to be a mixture though often there will be three main categories:

1   Content-based objectives, including subject specific objectives.
2   Objectives, which seek to extend students' historical understanding.
3   Objectives relating to the students' ability to organise and communicate.

WWW
There is a detailed objectives/outcomes 'bank' available and exemplar lesson plans on
http://www.routledge.com/textbooks/9780415370240

Tracking an objective through a lesson

Even the most precise objectives are of little use if they are not related to what actually happens in the classroom, so it is important that your lesson plan shows exactly where a specified objective will be addressed within the lesson. A common practice is to indicate alongside your description of the phase of a lesson, which objective is being met at that point.

Assessing the objectives

A characteristic of most objectives, though not all, is that they are capable of being assessed. Assessment is a vast, complex and at times in history, inexact activity. It is important as part of your lesson planning that you think through how you intend to assess whether your students have achieved the desired outcomes, although this will not necessarily be possible within the lesson itself but quite often after written work has been completed. In the later discussion of lesson evaluations, on p. 24, we will return to planning for assessing the quality of the learning achieved in lessons, remedying limited achievement and reinforcing what has been learned.

In Activity 3.3, you are asked to consider the merits and limitations of four approaches to evaluating your objectives.

Activity 3.3 Evaluating the achievement of your objectives

It is tempting to make assumptions about the extent to which your pupils achieve what you intended. Build into a succession of lessons that you have been asked to give the four examples of assessment and for each consider their merits and limitations as a means of finding out if your objectives have been achieved. Discuss with your mentor your conclusions about their reliability and validity.

1   Whole class question and answer in the end of lesson plenary.

_____

_____

_____

2   Pupils creating diagrammatic or pictorial representations of knowledge and concepts, e.g. mind maps, graphs.

_____

_____

_____

3   Written work: answering questions in simple sentences using information in the textbook or a duplicated sheet.

_____

_____

_____

4   Written work: writing an imaginative piece in which they write from the point of view of a participant in an event.

_____

_____

_____

MEDIUM-TERM PLANNING

Following a successful first placement, most trainee teachers will be hoping to develop their medium-term planning skills at their next school. A longer second placement offers the opportunity to attempt planning in a more 'joined-up' way, employing a greater range of different activities within each lesson than you may have delivered at your first school. Medium-term planning demands that you craft separate lessons within a cohesive unit that also fits neatly into the school's overarching long-term plan for the Key Stage which might also encompass the wider issues of literacy, numeracy, ICT, assessment for learning and citizenship. You will also use a variety of strategies to allow all pupils to achieve their best work. Increasingly the focus shifts towards the quality of learning taking place in your classroom as well as your own performance (see Activity 3.4). Quality medium-term planning balances the need to maintain the interest of your students while adding rigour to your teaching.

> **Activity 3.4** Matching content to key elements
>
> Using the History department's programme of content to be covered at KS3, try to identify which topics would be most suitable for the delivery of which Key Elements. When completed, compare with the department's actual scheme. Discuss the results with your mentor and state the reasons for your choice.

The example of medium-term planning is a five-lesson unit based on Henry II and Becket. The main question the unit seeks to answer is the apparently enigmatic 'Why did Hugh and Edward come to blows on 29 December 1170?' What do you need to consider when faced with the planning of such a unit?

1 How will you decide what to teach?

As a trainee teacher there will be necessary constraints on what topics you are asked to teach. The degree of choice you have will vary between placements. Some departments may be heavily prescriptive, others more flexible. Some will allow you greater freedom of choice in your planning in the later stages of the course. Some may invite you to contribute a new unit for the department in your final placement. More often there is some flexibility given within a prescribed topic. You may be able to conflate or intersperse several topics as is the case in our exemplar material.

Here the prescription is the story of Henry II and Becket to be used to develop the pupils' understanding of historical interpretations. In order to appreciate fully the subtleties and intricacies of the relationship between Henry II and Thomas Becket, the pupils are offered a look at the contrasting lifestyles of monks and knights in the twelfth century. In this way, two other frequently taught topics are also covered and in a way that shows the influence of their lifestyles on their interpretation of an event. This justifies the length of time spent concentrating on the unit by widening the scope of the content and learning objectives.

2 What will the outcomes be?

When planning a unit of work, the long-term objectives can then be broken down into short-term 'steps along the way' which become the objectives for each lesson. Often, there will be one or two over-arching objectives for the unit, and then accompanying objectives for the individual lesson.

At first glance, this enquiry would appear to be based on the key historical skill of causation and that concept is involved. Indeed, the pupils must acquire a sound appreciation of how the long-term, short-term and trigger events contribute to Becket's death if they are to address what is the central thrust of the unit – interpretations. Such is the nature of studying history that it is very unlikely you will be able to isolate one Key Element and that has implications for assessment as well. The two men named in the question are Hugh of Horsea – one of the killer knights, and Edward Grim – the monk who witnessed the event. Year 7 pupils can often recognise that it is possible to have different versions of the same event, but find it harder *to begin to explain how and why these differences can arise.* In Year 7, therefore, this enquiry clearly shows how two characters interpret a series of events differently because of their friendships, lifestyles and beliefs. Thus the outcomes sought can be summarised as follows:

That by the end of this unit the pupils should be able to understand that:

(i)   historical events can be interpreted in different ways and
(ii) such differences will often depend upon (a) the author's background and (b) the evidence to which the author has access.

The final task, seeking to reinforce the desired outcomes, concentrates on literacy and pupils' listening skills and assessment for learning because they arise naturally from the planned series of lessons.

3 Where will I find my resources?

Selective use of textbooks can be an easy way of structuring and resourcing a unit of work. Increasingly textbooks offer chapters that provide work for several lessons and have a major task at the end, and that are designed to target specific Key Elements throughout the chapter (see Activity 3.5). However, if the guidelines suggested thus far are used, then it is rare to find a textbook that can wholly address your objectives without compromising coherence. Often pre-designed worksheets and sections of textbooks can contribute in a meaningful way to a unit, but teachers should be wary of using a favourite activity or source when it does not completely meet the needs of the lesson sequence. In these cases, it is better to design new worksheets and trawl the Internet for fresh source material (see Chapters 7 and 9 in this book for guidance). By creating your own resources, you can be sure that they comprehensively meet your objectives and have increased ownership over your planning. Although creating resources and photocopying can be draining on time and have financial implications within departments, a well-presented worksheet or laminated card sort can be reused. Careful use of technology can also increase the lifespan of a resource. Additionally, always be on the look-out for 'bits and pieces' – cartoons, newspaper articles, video extracts, which will make an impact.

Activity 3.5 Planning with a textbook

Choose a textbook with a double-page coverage of a topic. Read the page carefully and then consider the following:

1   What you want the pupils to gain from the material displayed on these pages in terms of (i) knowledge; (ii) skills; and (iii) an aspect of a Key Element.
2   When and how you could use the text in the lesson.
3   What you need to do to supplement and adapt the textbook information.
4   What do you recognise as being the dangers and possible pitfalls involved in using the textbook in your lessons?

There are many good quality resources available to assist teaching the story of Becket and Henry II, such as play scripts and chronology activities (see Activity 3.6). Most textbooks offer source material and a basic outline of the events; this lesson sequence draws on one of these accounts and uses a variety of textbooks for the research phase of Lesson Two. However, most other resources were created within the department for this unit and its specifically intended outcomes. Principal among these were the 'Voice of the Past' taped accounts. These were a series of pre-recorded imaginary conversations between Hugh and Edward that narrate the highs and lows of the relationship between Henry II and Thomas Becket at key intervals from 1162 when Becket became Archbishop, until his murder in 1170. Hugh and Edward's accounts contain obvious bias in attitude and language and pupils are regularly asked 'How would Hugh or Edward explain this event?' and pupils are constantly referred back to the idea that the 'friendship' between Hugh and Henry II, and Edward and Becket, colours the interpretations of the events described. Another important resource was the story board. From this pupils examine a hypothetical 'day in the life' of a medieval knight.

Activity 3.6 Investigating resources

1   Collect together a range of textbooks, worksheets and other resources on one topic. Sort the resources into piles determined by the skill that they are focused on. Does your topic seem to lend itself to one specific skill? Is this the skill that you would have chosen?

2   Using your collection of resources, make a checklist of the characteristics of a good classroom resource, to be used when you create resources.

_____   _____

_____   _____

_____   _____

_____   _____

_____   _____

4 How can I provide quality individual lessons as well as give coherence across the unit?

Try to remember that each lesson should build on the previous one, in terms of knowledge, skill and progress towards the end task. Both teacher and pupils should be constantly aware of the long-term objectives throughout the teaching of the unit – and the teacher should make it clear to the pupils how each activity and piece of information contributes to the end product. The exemplar lessons rely heavily on the reinforcement of the characters' identities, their allegiances, biased opinions and reasons for these at the start and end of most lessons. Whilst designing the separate lessons, teachers must be conscious of the activities that they are using. A delicate balance between providing new, exciting tasks each time you ask the pupils to do something, and giving them the chance to practise and revisit certain tasks must be struck. The exemplar unit recycles the 'listening comprehension' idea to foster good listening skills in younger students while exploring different ways of learning factual information. Yet the challenge remains that, however engrossing the activity, it is important pupils see how it contributes to their historical understanding. Use of the starter and plenary activities to remind pupils of their progress within a series of lessons is particularly useful in maintaining the flow of a longer lesson sequence. Teachers have to consider how factual knowledge is to be retained from one lesson to the next; it is not always appropriate or possible to revisit key information as a class. Activity 3.7 is useful in creating an ideas bank of task ideas.

Activity 3.7 Compiling an ideas bank

1   During your placements, keep a list of innovative task ideas that you come across within your department.

2   Ask colleagues with other subject specialisms to suggest ideas that work in their departments. Can they be adapted to be used in history lessons? Be careful to make sure that these tasks meet history learning objectives once they are altered.

5 How will you assess the pupils' progress?

From the initial starting point of planning a unit, it is helpful to be aware of what piece or pieces of work you will assess and how. Try to be imaginative here; essays and formal GCSE-style responses to historical sources need to be practised, but mix in presentations using ICT, newspaper articles, and more innovative ideas such as asking pupils to judge a 'competition' for most efficient industry in 1850, or provide 'interview questions' for key historical figures after famous events to elicit their actions and explanations with pupils responding 'in character'.

Just as the content and the treatment of the main concept are developed over the five lessons, so also coherence is developed by anticipating the final piece of work with which the pupils will conclude the unit. Once you have a clear idea what this will be, it is easier to plan individual lessons that will allow students to practise the skills required in the final piece or build sections towards it. Writing Edward's version of the murder in the cathedral at the end of the unit provides an opportunity for all pupils to show how much they have learned over the series of lessons, but this is built on the foundations of previous oral attempts to explain events from Edward's point of view. Your school and departmental assessment policies will have a major impact on the number and type of assessment opportunities needed within each unit of work. However, you should not aim to provide comprehensive written feedback for every activity that pupils undertake. Focus instead *on those activities that directly show a pupil's competence in the dominant Key Element* within the lesson sequence and provide clear guidance for the pupils on how their work has impressed you, and how they can further improve next time, adding marks, grades or levels as is appropriate within your school context. Over the course of a unit of work, it is appropriate to provide informal assessment comments to indicate how a pupil is progressing towards acquiring the skills that will be tested in the final piece and to make certain that every pupil has sufficient factual knowledge to use as a basis to demonstrate those higher-order skills, in this case, the explanation of interpretations. Thus, in the final lesson, the pupils are to write the priest's version of events and try to explain them from his perspective based on evidence available to him, such as information he had gained from his conversations with Becket.

THE EXEMPLAR LESSONS

Enquiry question: 'Why did Hugh and Edward come to blows on the 29 December 1170?' The five lessons, given to a mixed ability Year 7 class, each lasted one hour.

> **www**
>
> For the curriculum material associated with these lessons, see:
>
> http://www.routledge.com/textbooks/9780415370240

First lesson

The pupils were introduced to Hugh and Edward. The pupil activities included: identifying the jobs shown on two pictures of a monk and a knight; using comprehension sheets as they listened to a tape of conversations and interviews involving Hugh and Edward; studying an A3 storyboard about Hugh's life and answering a question sheet about Hugh's life and finally doing a differentiated wordsearch.

Second lesson

The lifestyle of monks and priests is considered. Pupil tasks included the structured creation using textbooks of a storyboard about Edward to match that of Hugh. This anticipates and prepares the pupils for the written task at the end of the unit.

Third lesson

The question 'Who were Henry II and Becket?' is introduced. Pupil tasks included making notes as a tape is played of a conversation between Hugh and Edward, giving information about Henry and Becket; discussing an OHT showing Henry's aims; reading and answering questions using an information sheet. There was an important plenary on the fall-out between Henry and Becket asking how Hugh and Edward in turn might explain it. The pupils were encouraged to look for different interpretations and to explain them.

Fourth lesson

Why Becket and Henry fell out. The pupil activities included listening to further information from another taped conversation between Hugh and Edward; making a list of reasons for the fall-out; looking at a textbook's account of the event; using and making a graph, which plotted the changing relationship between the king and his archbishop and discussing further Hugh and Edward's different explanation of events covered so far. Using graphs is a very useful way of transferring or summarising information, offering a welcome alternative to a written record.

Final lesson

The pupils learn how the story ends for the first time. By listening to Hugh's pre-recorded 'voice from the past', pupils learn that Thomas Becket is murdered and that Edward is injured. Hugh's account weaves the facts of 29 December together with his own reasons for attacking the archbishop. Hugh's account relies heavily on past occasions where Henry II has been displeased with Becket and explains his violence with the argument that it was ordered by the king. It purports to have been written one day after the murder. The lesson plan directs the teacher to ask pupils to examine the style and content of Hugh's account in preparation for writing their own account from Edward's point of view. Pupils with a wide range of abilities can access this task when the guidance points are reduced and all pupils enjoy writing in detail about Becket's death. It is not a struggle to get pupils to put pen to paper when they are describing such a gruesome event! The final task draws heavily on assessment for learning techniques and pupils use the structure of Hugh's account as a writing frame for their own.

PLANNING FOR LESSON EVALUATION

It is important to evaluate lessons primarily on the basis of whether the students learned what you wanted them to, rather than whether they behaved. Referring back to the five stages of planning and comparing your intentions with the actual outcomes of the lesson sequence is one way of evaluating your teaching. After reviewing each stage thoroughly, you should be able to articulate the progress made by your students, why they made it (or didn't), the next steps for this class and how you will use what you have learned in future planning for all your classes. There will be times when it is helpful to concentrate on one particular aspect of your teaching or one feature of the lesson for your evaluation.

Activity 3.8 will help you to consider the key questions that you might ask to evaluate the planning of a unit.

> ### Activity 3.8 Evaluating the planning
>
> The aim of this activity is to help you explore the processes by which you can evaluate the effectiveness of your planning with the use of the unit described in the chapter.
>
> 1   Devise a set of specific questions you would ask about the planning of this unit. You might consider:
>
> (i)   the claims made for the pupils' learning;
>
> _____
>
> (ii)   the structure of the unit, its coherence and development;
>
> _____
>
> (iii)   the requirements made of the pupils;
>
> _____
>
> (iv)   the resources;
>
> _____
>
> (v)   the opportunities for formative assessment.
>
> _____
>
> 2   What would be the assessment criteria for the final piece of work?
>
> _____

SUMMARY

Good lesson planning usually brings its rewards in terms of successful lessons, although there is no guarantee of success every time. Yet lesson planning is time-consuming and the more you can utilise strategies to reduce time, the better it will be. Trainees have found it valuable to make a lesson plan template, particularly where plans can be adapted for different abilities; some recommend the use of autotext on MS Word. It is advisable to keep any content notes separate from your lesson plans, which usually can be limited to one page of A4. Other strategies that are helpful include keeping your evaluation of previous lessons to hand, planning schemes of work as fully as the information given to you allows including ideas for possible activities and likely resources. This will reduce the time spent on the individual plans. Finally, even though historians are great accumulators, always keep plans of successful lessons beyond your training year. They can often be adapted for future lessons.

ACKNOWLEDGEMENT

Thanks are due to Matthew Little, John Kirkham and Lisa Whitby for their help in the creation of the resources, used to teach the story of Becket and Henry II.

FURTHER READING

Lomas T. (1990) *Teaching and Assessing Historical Understanding*, Historical Association.

Steele, I. (1976) *Developments in History Teaching*, Chapter 4.

The *Teaching History* problem page also has useful discussions on lesson objectives in issues 100 (2000) and 104 (2001).

Chapter 4 Learning strategies and approaches

SIMON GOODWIN

INTRODUCTION

The aim of this chapter is to help you design learning activities for your first lessons. It should encourage you to experiment with different methods and assess their suitability for different individuals, classes and topics. Exemplar material involving the First World War has been used, which could be modified for those topics you are asked to teach. Towards the end of the chapter there are some more advanced activities that you might like to try later, all of which complement the discussion covered in Chapter 4 of *Learning to Teach History in the Secondary School*, 2nd edn, Routledge, 2001.

This chapter will consider three basic activities familiar to most history lessons:

- Reading/research/exposition
- Questioning/discussion
- Presentation (oral or written).

Chapter aims

By the end of the chapter you should be able to:

- design learning activities for your first lessons;
- apply guidance on the creation of appropriate materials for reading in the classroom;
- understand the strengths and limitations of a range of approaches involving the use of reading;
- take steps to develop your exposition skills;
- employ a range of questions in your teaching and use them in a variety of ways;
- understand the strategies for successful group work;
- use a variety of approaches to written tasks including the use of mind maps.

Think of any lesson you have observed so far. Frequently, the class will have read a text or listened to a story or looked at a picture, then discussed it before doing some writing about it. Each activity could be for individuals, groups or whole classes. Before you experiment with more complex teaching strategies, you need to feel confident in managing these activities. Do not worry about 'starters' and 'plenaries' (where pupils review their learning) at this stage. If you put these three basic activities together, you have a sound 'bread and butter' lesson. Your early priority should be to experiment with a variety of simple strategies and find the ones with which you are most comfortable. Every teacher has a battery of teaching methods upon which to draw in any given lesson situation.

The following activities are designed to help you develop a range of teaching methods.

READING/EXPOSITION/RESEARCH

In order to discuss the more interesting questions raised by the study of history, students have to acquire some basic knowledge first. For the most part, this means reading a text, watching a film or listening to a teacher exposition. The success of this activity will make or break your lesson.

Reading

Reading activities can be crucial to the success of your lesson. Early on, it is easier to rely on a textbook narrative. However, re-typing the narrative can simplify both language and layout and can help you to take ownership of the detail. The following guidance will help:

1   Avoid over-loading a page with information.
2   Add a clear title and make it a question (thus emphasising the aim of your lesson).
3   Add an illustration.
4   At all times remember: the simpler the text, the fewer problems, interruptions and awkward questions you will have to deal with.
5   Tasks should be 'boxed off' separately.
6   Each question should be short, clear and should give an indication of the detail needed in the answer.
7   Finally, one blindingly obvious (but often ignored) tip is to attempt the tasks yourself before teaching the lesson.

> **WWW**
>
> For trench warfare exemplar material to support the activities see
> http://www.routledge.com/textbooks/9780415370240

Try the different tasks in Activity 4.1, which are designed to encourage you to experiment with different approaches to reading.

Exposition

Exposition or story telling is an aspect of learning history that all students enjoy, whatever their age or ability. Telling a story without a text can be an effective way to keep a class focused, involved and stimulated, without putting stress on their reading skills. However, this can be a nerve-wracking experience for the beginning teacher trainee:

1   If students have a written text to refer to, this will give you reassurance. If you feel you are losing your thread, you can take the students back to the text.
2   You will feel much more comfortable if you have a series of pictures around which to build your story. This could be in the form of overhead transparencies (OHTs) or PowerPoint slides.
3   Lowering the classroom lights will help focus their attention on the visuals and on you. Furthermore, they will signify a move to a different type of activity.
4   Move around the room, to emphasise the movement of the narrative but stay absolutely still to emphasise the key events.

Activity 4.1 Evaluating approaches to reading

For this Activity, you are asked to experiment with the three reading activities.

1   *Either* prepare some reading material on topics you have been asked to teach to KS3 classes. It would be helpful if you could use the same material with each class but this is unlikely. The material should include a combination of text and tasks using the principles set out on p. 28. The text should have about 300 words of detailed, factual prose, highlighting key words. Add a picture and then include a set of short, clear, mainly comprehension questions.
     Or, should circumstances permit, you could use the First World War exemplar material available on: http://routledge.com/textbooks/9780415370240

2   Using your information sheet, experiment with each of the three approaches described below:

   A. *Try reading the extract to the class or asking for volunteers to read. This is a very common method of engaging with a text. Then, ask the questions from section (1) one by one. Students should put their hand up to speak and be silent until called upon. Be firm on this but don't be disheartened if some students don't comply at first. Take volunteers at first, then try to involve some other students who seem more reluctant. This will take about 5 minutes.*

   B. *Ask another class to read the story individually in silence or at least quietly. Give them a precise time limit, for example, 3 minutes. Tell them that after 3 minutes you are going to ask them about the story. Tell them to put their hand up if they find a difficult word. Then, repeat the questioning process. A variation on this task could be to ask students to read in pairs, and thus support each other.*

   C. *Try repeating the above activity again, but this time give every student a coloured pen or pencil. This time they have 3 minutes to highlight all the problems of trench life that they can find. Alternatively, they can make a list of problems in the back of their exercise books, on paper, or even on a mini white board. Varying the method will keep their interest in the task.*

1   What were the advantages and limitations of each of the three approaches?

     _____

     _____

2   Were there any particular reasons for the weakness of any one approach?

     _____

     _____

3   Consider which approach is the most suitable for the classes you are currently working with. Discuss your conclusions with your mentor.

     _____

     _____

Activity 4.1 *continued*

4 Are there any other approaches to reading in the classroom, which you have observed? How do they compare with the three approaches above?

_____

_____

5 Changing the tone and volume of your voice will add further emphasis. Once you have their attention, try lowering your voice so they have to strain just a little to hear you. Every so often, pause to ask a question.

Activity 4.2 encourages you to develop your exposition skills.

Activity 4.2 Developing your exposition skills

In this Activity you are invited to make a presentation/exposition to a class directly, that is without reference to a text. So, you will find it easier to develop these skills if this is accompanied by a picture or diagram on an OHT or a PowerPoint slide, the content of which encourages you *to move about* as your narrative unravels. The following list merely illustrates the vast variety of possibilities for such energetic exposition. Consider the possible impact of: attacking a medieval castle; the feudal system; various execution scenes including the guillotine; battle plans; road building; the Elizabethan theatre; four-crop rotation; cartoons; cross-sections, e.g. ships and for the exemplar material on the website, First World War trenches and, if you are up to it, Newcomen's Steam Engine.

1 Select an appropriate picture or diagram.
2 List the key features and key words you will wish to emphasise.
3 Think through how you will try to make a physical impact with your exposition. For example, with the cross-section of the trench, the depth of the trench was roughly the same height as a classroom ceiling. You could use a wall for your pararpet and a chair for your firestep. All through your story the students can see an actual trench on the screen. Don't be afraid to stand on a chair or point at an imaginary barbed wire. As you explain each element of the trench, ask them what its purpose was.
4 Then consider:

(i) Was this more or less successful than using a text-book description?

_____

_____

(ii) What might be the strengths and limitations of both approaches?

_____

_____

Research

Research in the sense used here means finding out facts. This often means the students finding information from textbooks, worksheets, library books or the Internet. This is most commonly used as a homework task, but it can be a valid classroom activity, if you have the resources to hand. The danger here is that students merely regurgitate material without understanding it or even that they find the task too demanding. Three strategies will help you here. First, pose questions to be researched rather than topics or headings. Second, give one accessible text as an example but make it clear that good researchers will look at more than one source of information. Third, ask students to present their information in a different format. This could be a mind map (explained later on in this chapter), a table or a diagram. This means they have to process the information to transfer it to the new format.

QUESTIONING/DISCUSSION

If you have carried out the above activities then you have already questioned a class and managed a short discussion. You will have observed many questioning activities, but do not be fooled into thinking that this is an easy skill to master. History teachers are natural questioners and know through experience what works and what does not.

Developing your questioning technique

There are a few principles to bear in mind here. First, you should ask a mixture of 'open' and 'closed' questions. Closed questions are usually factual and have one answer. For example, when studying the First World War trenches: *What was a duckboard for?* or *What was trench foot?* Open questions are usually more reflective, open to debate and need to be answered at greater length, with supporting evidence. For example: *What would have been the most hated aspect of trench life?* All classes appreciate a mixture. Closed questions build confidence and help to get everyone involved. Open questions involve higher-order thinking.

Second, you should aim for a mixture of 'volunteers' and 'conscripts' to answer your questioners. Volunteers are enthusiastic and need to feel involved. Conscripts need and deserve the opportunity to join in too. Try to involve all areas of the classroom, both genders and all abilities. Third, think about pace and pauses. Some learners revel in a quick-fire question and answer. Others need time to reflect before raising their hand. After asking a question, get into the habit of counting to two or three before taking a response.

At first, you might like to prepare a list of questions to ask, or at least to fall back upon if needed. This will help you to think about the important issue of sequencing questions. However, do not be afraid to let the class lead you away from your script. That will not be a problem if you stick to the above principles. You will also find that student participation will increase if you provide a stimulus. This could be a picture or diagram, for example.

Activity 4.3 has questioning activities for you to try (the First World War trenches again provide examples).

Activity 4.3   Encouraging question and answer

For this Activity you are asked to experiment with the following three questioning activities. Each time consider the strategies and weaknesses of each approach. However, if there are weaknesses, consider why. Different activities may suit different individuals, classes and situations:

1   Select a picture, map or diagram, which is not too cluttered but which has enough information to be the basis for several questions. You could use your choice for Activity 4.2, applying what is exemplified in the First World War trench cross-section to your own material.

2   Give the students 1 minute to make a list or a mind map of the trench problems in the back of their book or on paper. Start the discussion by asking some closed factual questions about trenches and then allow them to share their ideas. Finally, ask them to make a judgement of the worst problems.

3   Alternatively, give the students 23 minutes to draw and label the diagram of the trench from memory on a mini-white board. Then start the discussion as above. With a white board it is easier to ask students to put ideas in a rank or chronological order.

4   Finally, re-enact your exposition on trenches (with the chair, etc.) but this time ask the students what you are doing or pointing at.

5   (i)   Which approach engaged most learners?

_____

_____

(ii)   Which approach made classroom management easier?

_____

_____

Encouraging question and answer

Once you feel confident with these activities, try to use oral questioning to access some higher-order thinking skills. Most of your questions will probably have been factual, descriptive, recall questions. You might like to try the following (dependent on your lesson objectives) and in order of difficulty:

Inference	*What can we learn about . . .?*
Comparison	*How are x and y similar/different?*
Categorisation	*Which causes are social/economic/ political factors?*
Analysis	*Which effect was the most important?*
Evaluation	*Why do historians disagree about this issue?*

Do not feel you have to use each style of question in one lesson. Pick and choose, but bear in mind the increasing difficulty.

STUDENT PRESENTATION (ORAL OR WRITTEN)

Many would argue that it is vital that you give students the opportunity to present their own response to the material you have given them. This could take many forms, some of which will be discussed in later chapters. Here, we will concentrate on the most simple – note-taking and oral presentations. Bear in mind that some students find *written work* boring, so aim for a variety of tasks and only ask for detail/length when it is appropriate for the task.

Look back at the examples of trench warfare tasks. What written activities could you ask the students to do? Many teachers would commonly ask students to write out answers to the questions. If you do this, ask students not to copy the question out but write all their answers in sentences. Give students an indication of the length of answer required. For example, 'write a paragraph' or 'explain your answer'. Note-taking can take many forms. However, if you just ask students to 'write up the information in your own words', without modelling, guidance and structure, it is likely that you will not get the response you want. Try the different written tasks in Activity 4.4.

Activity 4.4 Evaluating approaches to written tasks

The aim of this Activity is for you to analyse and evaluate a variety of alternative written tasks, all of them in common use in the history classroom.

For this exercise you could use the material you devised for Activity 4.1 or create new material from another topic. Use the principles in this chapter to help you to create your tasks using questions, structured notes and a cloze exercise. You may find the 3-part exemplar material on questioning on the website helpful for this task:

1 Ask the students to write out the answers to the set of short questions based on the information sheet as exemplified in part (i). Ask the students not to copy the question out and to write their answers in sentences. Give them an indication of the length of the answer required such as 'write at least four lines', 'write a paragraph' or 'explain your answer'.

2 Ask the students to write out at least one sentence about each of the bullet points, which list details of the content of the infromation sheet, this time exemplified in part (ii). Note-taking can take many forms. However, if you ask the students to 'write up the information in your own words', it is unlikely you will get the response you want.

3 Ask the students to copy out a cloze paragraph, see part (iii), and fill in the gaps using the words from the word box. Ask them either to underline the missing words or to write them in a different colour.

4 (i) Evaluate the strengths and weaknesses of each task.
   (ii) How would you use these tasks at different times with different classes?
   (iii) How could the tasks be combined to provide for individual differences?

5 Discuss your conclusions with your mentor or Head of Department.

Using a mind map

Mind maps have already been mentioned in the chapter and deserve fuller treatment. A mind map is a more sophisticated learning tool and has a number of rules:

1 The title should be highlighted for emphasis.
2 All words should be written on the line, so long words need long lines.
3 Each word must be linked to another word or to the title. Students can also add their own symbols or illustrations or use colour.
4 Mind maps can serve several functions. They can be short-hand notes. If you do this, make sure the students include specific information such as proper nouns, statistics, etc.

Second, they can be used as a plan for a piece of extended writing. Students read through the chains of words to create sentences. Third, they can be used as a revision tool. Students read the mind maps aloud to a partner and then try to re-create them on a blank sheet of paper. This is particularly effective because the learner reads, speaks and writes the material in one activity, which aids the process of memorisation. You could combine all these functions in Activity 4.5.

Activity 4.5 Using a mind map

The aim of this Activity is to analyse and evaluate how mind maps can be used in place of traditional written notes, how they can be used to commit information to memory and how they can be used to plan more extended written work:

1 Study the mind map below, noting how it develops.
2 Replace the title 'Trenches' with that of your own topic and your detail for that of the exemplar material, which follows.
3 Give students a blank piece of paper and a copy of the word box. Write 'Trenches' on the white board and ask students to do the same on their sheet. Ask them for a word that describes what 'trenches' were like. They may say 'cramped' or 'waterlogged'. Add the word to the mind map. Next ask them whether 'trench foot' should link to 'cramped' or 'waterlogged' and add their choice to the map. Now they can see the rules of mind-mapping they can work individually for five minutes to complete their own mind map using all 20 words. Emphasise that the maps are individual and that there are no right or wrong answers.
4 Now ask the students to read their mind maps aloud to themselves or to their neighbour (in turn). Emphasise that this is a vital part of the process. Give them 2 minutes for this. They can now either write out their plans in sentences and paragraphs or they can try to commit it to memory. To do this, ask students to turn their sheets of paper over to the blank side. Give them 5 minutes to recreate their mind map, aiming for 20 words. You will find that all the class will be able to recreate at least 75 per cent of the map.
5 (i)   Does the mind map approach suit all pupils?
   (ii) What are the strengths and limitations of mind-mapping when compared to traditional note-taking?

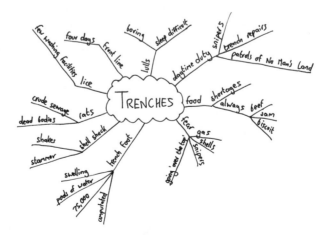

Figure 4.1 Mind map of trenches in the First World War

> **www**
>
> Other mind map activities may be seen at:
>
> httpl/:www.routledge.com/textbooks/9780415370240
>
> or at: http://www.mindmap.com

Many trainees shy away from *oral presentations* by the students because they fear losing control of a group. You may be surprised at how attentively students listen to their peers. You will also find that some reluctant or challenging individuals suddenly start to shine. Activity 4.6 enables you to experiment with this strategy with classes with whom you feel comfortable.

Activity 4.6   Using presentations

1   Make a 2-minute presentation to the class on any topic, even a non-historical one. Write a list of bullet points on prompt cards and use a visual aid. Ask the class to tell you what made the presentation go well. They may highlight eye contact, the cue cards and the visual aid. You have now modelled a simple presentation style.

2   Divide the class into groups of two, three or four. You will achieve better results if you choose the groups. Ask their regular teacher for advice. Assign a topic to each group and give them time to research it (see research section). Give each group at least one OHT around which to build their presentation and give them a time limit. They will want to work at length on this but 45 minutes should be enough. With 5 minutes to go, ask each group to do a rehearsal.

3   It will take at least 45 minutes for eight groups of four to make a 2-minute presentation. After each one ask the others to give a strength of each presentation. You could even design a prompt sheet for them to fill in.

4   (i)   What practical problems did you encounter in organising this activity?
    (ii) How could these problems be anticipated or avoided in future?
    (iii) How could you encourage the pupils to assess each other's work?

Group work

Group work can be a thorny topic for trainees. The benefits of group work are often heard: it encourages co-operation, negotiating, builds language skills and provides an environment for providing for individual differences. In practice, the thought of encouraging pupil chatter and movement around the room can deter the trainee. Here are some practical tips for successful group work:

1   Choose the composition of groups yourself instead of letting pupils choose. They may complain at first but will soon just get on with things. Better still, put them into groups before entering the room, or have place cards on desks.

2   Consider how to create good working groups, with mixtures of ability, temperament and work ethic. Effective group selection can transform the atmosphere in a classroom.

3   Start with small groups (pairs, for example) before getting more ambitious.

4   Give groups clear instructions, better still, assign every group member to a particular task (e.g.: chair, scribe, reporter, etc.).

5   Pupils will work with more enthusiasm if they have individual roles, and if they can contribute to a whole class activity. For example, to gather evidence for a trial of Charles I.

SUMMARY

The aim of this chapter has been to help you find a basic teaching style that suits you. By experimenting with a variety of reading, discussion and writing activities you should be able to see which activities suit different situations and classes. Your students will appreciate variety in the tasks you ask them to complete.

As you move through your training course you may want to revisit this chapter and re-assess some of the approaches.

Ten tried and tested tips from this chapter (in no particular order) are:

1   Choose short, simple texts for students to read.
2   For higher-order questions, ask students to rank factors or judge importance.
3   To judge relative importance, ask students to find links between factors.
4   If you design a task, do it yourself first.
5   Use pictures for exposition.
6   Collect interesting anecdotes and quirky facts for your expositions.
7   Don't worry about 'starters and plenaries' at first. Concentrate on the three types of activities discussed in this chapter.
8   Use the same questioning principles for oral and written work.
9   Keep questions short and make it clear what length of response is required.
10   Consider the use of a set of mini white boards. These are A4 sized double-sided white boards for individual students to use, with a conventional white board marker. These can transform group work, starter activities and essay planning.

FURTHER READING

Counsell, C. (1997) *Analytical and Discursive Writing in History at Key Stage 3*, Historical Association.

Lewis, M. and Wray, D. (1997) *Extending Literacy: Children Reading and Writing Non-Fiction*, London: Routledge.

McCully, A. (1997) 'Key questions, planning and extended writing', *Teaching History*, 89, October, 31–5.

Please also see the bibliography on http://www.routledge.com/textbooks/9780415370240

Chapter 5   Role play as active history

STEVE GUSCOTT

INTRODUCTION

This chapter considers one way of enriching the teaching of history – role play. For the purposes of this chapter, role play means the active engagement of both teacher and pupils in the interpretation of the past. Despite the promotion of 'active history' in the past twenty years, role play remains an under-utilised method of delivering history. Much of this stems from a perception that 'acting out' an aspect of history is a distraction from the development of pupils' historical understanding. In addition, some teachers may believe that preparation and classroom management issues make drama a time-consuming luxury. These concerns, it will be shown, can be avoided if lessons and activities are properly prepared and pupils understand why they are engaged in a particular activity.

Some obvious concerns that trainee teachers might feel about role play are:

- pressure on organisational and classroom management skills – 'kids can go bonkers';
- managing different groups at the same time;
- the assessment of pupils using this approach, that is, *all* pupils;
- ensuring that pupils learn from the experience and that it adds to their historical knowledge and understanding;
- time to prepare properly.

As a trainee teacher, you may feel reluctant to consider role plays. Quite rightly you might feel that lesson planning, classroom management and developing pupils' historical understanding should be your main priorities. This chapter, however, will argue that role play can enhance your teaching. The use of drama can stimulate 'problem' classes. The paradox is that, especially for trainees, discipline considerations might deter the use of the very approach which could well produce a positive change of attitude. It can facilitate the understanding of difficult subject-specific concepts, improve extended writing across the ability range, raise the status of history in schools, and make the subject both challenging and fun.

Chapter aims

By the end of this chapter you should be able to:

- understand how the use of role play offers opportunities for pupils who respond to different ways of learning including kinaesthetic learners;
- be able to identify opportunities for role play within the history curriculum;

• be able to design learning materials for the successful use of role plays including improvisation, scripted plays and teacher-led activities;
• link role play activities to the assessment of pupils.

PLANNING FOR ROLE PLAY

One of the most common misconceptions about role play is that it needs to be an 'all singing, all dancing' festival of active drama, with all pupils having to write and act their parts. It does not, as may be seen in the simple use of role play used in Chapter 2 and in the excellent, short sharp 'practical demonstration' type activities advocated by Ian Luff (2000). Before you plan any role play, though, it would be useful to consider some basic guidelines. As outlined in *Learning to Teach History in the Secondary School*, 2nd edn, Routledge, 2001, pp. 75–6, subject knowledge, preparation time, organisation and follow-up work are crucial.

Consider Activity 5.1. This depth of planning is vital before any role play activity is attempted within the classroom. Whatever format the activity is going to take, the use of drama should never be *unplanned* – both pupils and teachers should be made fully aware of the purpose of what they are doing. Active History lessons should be like any other history activity – clearly focused, tied to what pupils already know and understand, with concise aims and objectives and a way of helping pupils to make further progress.

Role play can take a variety of different forms –

• *Role play as consolidator of knowledge* – pre-written plays, full drama work.
• *Role play as fun – teaching historical skills* – invigorating source work/interpretations/ significance activities.
• *Role play as assessment* – mock trials, debates, pupil-created plays.
• *Role play as deliverer of knowledge and understanding* – teacher-led role play activities.

The rest of this chapter will consider each of these role play styles in turn.

Activity 5.1 Planning for role play over two lessons

Think of a topic that you are due to teach either at Key Stage 3 or Key Stage 4. How could you transform that topic into a vehicle for role play? Some questions to consider are:

• What are the learning objectives?
• What will the role play be about?
• What form will the role play take – play, debate, discussion?
• What will pupils need to know and understand before they do the activity?
• Will the whole class be involved or just a selection of pupils?
• What resources will pupils need to prepare for the activity?
• How long will they need to prepare?
• How long will the role play take?
• What will pupils who are not involved be doing while preparation/ performance is taking place?
• Will the role play be tied to assessment?

The proforma will help you to work out where you might consider using role play in the classroom.

Unit of work	Lesson objective	Type of role play	Characters/scenes to be written	Resources	Assessment focus

ROLE PLAY AS CONSOLIDATOR OF KNOWLEDGE – DRAMA

Role play can achieve a high impact when pupils know and understand what historical characters are doing and why they are doing it. In this sense, it consolidates knowledge. Historical characters, events, turning points and entire epochs can be brought alive. Understanding of previous work in a unit can be tested and challenged, and pupils' interest can be reawakened and reinvigorated.

One option is to involve the whole class in acting out a pre-written role play. Crucially, this does not have to mean weeks of preparation, costume creation and countless rehearsals. As a trainee, you might adopt a gradualist approach in which for your first use of a pre-written play the pupils read their parts sitting in their usual places. After that, in many cases, all it needs is a large space that can be created in any classroom by putting chairs and tables to the side. A few props and an imaginative use of space will do the rest. In my experience, pupils relish turning the room into a live theatre.

Pre-written role plays do exist. Consider a unit that many teachers find hard to teach – the English Civil War. The unit contains a number of concepts (Puritanism, royalism, parliamentarianism, divine right) that pupils often have difficulties in fully understanding. The Schools History Project has a role play that has always worked brilliantly in my experience – The Trial of Charles I (Shephard and Moore, 1995). It has four simple scenes, with a variety of characters both high and low, and conveys simply the story of Charles I's trial. The lesson plan below suggests how it could be used.

Lesson Plan: How fair was the trial of Charles I?

Aim: To enable pupils to reach a judgement on the justice of Charles I's trial. The lesson objectives should be:

- to enable pupils to show prior knowledge of Charles I's trial and execution;
- to enable pupils to understand the nature of Charles I's trial through active role play;
- to enable pupils to write a written summary of their own view of the fairness of the trial

Tasks

1   Recap previous knowledge of Charles I's trial and execution through question and answer.
2   Explain that pupils will be acting out the trial of Charles I. Explain the purpose of the activity. Why do *they* think that the activity will be useful?
3   Act out the trial – stop and start the activity, checking understanding, asking pupils to remember examples of fairness and unfairness.
4   Pupils then write their own summary of the trial, highlighting unfair aspects of the trial and explaining why they were unfair. An initial sentence could be modelled on the board, with a writing frame provided for lower attainers.
5   Plenary – question and answer – what have pupils learnt from the activity?

This sort of activity has a lot to recommend it. It does not require you to type or write it yourself, since you will have already given pupils a copy of the text. It is pre-written, and gives you the freedom to allocate parts as you see fit – the more demanding roles of John Bradshaw and Charles I through to witnesses like the maid with only one line. All ability ranges are catered for, and by stopping and starting the play with good questioning, understanding can be easily checked. The nature of the play engages pupils, as does the gory ending.

Equally important, though, is the tying of the activity to something relevant, in this case the production of a piece of writing on how fair the trial of Charles I really was. By engaging pupils in the past, they are better able to understand the detail of what happened, and can articulate their feelings about it. In this case, from my own experience, a lot of pupils end up changing their minds about Charles I's merits as a king.

Another excellent pre-written role play activity is Dale Banham and Ian Dawson's recreation of how William enacted the Norman Conquest (Banham and Dawson, 2000). This is a far more complex activity that is teacher-led and designed to develop an understanding of the following:

1 The pattern of rebellions against William and why the rebellions did not succeed.
2 The impact of the Normans on England, particularly the changes in landownership and why they came about.
3 How the English and the Normans felt about each other.

The room is divided up into different regions of the country, and the story of the Norman Conquest is gradually told, assessed and interpreted. In a debriefing, pupils consider what happened, why and when the rebellions against William failed.

Banham and Dawson also confirm why role play can work so well. First, it means better knowledge and understanding because 'pupils felt that they had learned more because they had both enjoyed the lesson and been actively involved'. Simply, it helped pupils to remember things much more clearly. Second, pupils learn in a number of different ways. Whether pupils are visual learners, auditory learners, or kinaesthetic learners, role plays such as this involve, motivate and improve learning (ibid., p. 16). Chapter 8 in this book discusses these types of learning.

More demanding are collaborations with other departments, especially the Drama Department. Clearly, this is not likely to be possible on a teaching placement, but a superb example of how a role play can motivate the whole school is that of the eighteenth-century enclosure of North Ferriby, Yorkshire, performed by South Hunsley School (see Snelson *et al.*, 2002, for a full description). It is also possible to pre-write a number of role plays on subjects as diverse as an imaginary trial of Henry VIII, the Terror, the assassination of Archduke Franz Ferdinand, and Jack the Ripper. Writing role plays can take time, but the teacher can control the content, the number of characters, the style of the play and the objective of the activity. A few jokes can be thrown in (as long as the pupils are made aware beforehand) but the principles outlined above are the same. A role play is a serious activity, that needs to be well planned, carefully monitored and have clearly defined aims and objectives.

Activity 5.2 can be used to work out the basis for your own pre-written role plays.

Activity 5.2 Designing a pre-written role play

Questions to address are:

1 What unit of work will the role play address?
2 What will pupils need to know and understand to access the role play?
3 What will be the lesson objective?
4 How many characters and scenes will there be? (Remember – pace and timing!)
5 What resources will I need to produce? Acetates/scripts for each pupil, etc.
6 How will I ensure that all pupils are included and participate in the activity?
7 How will I assess pupils' learning and understanding? Questioning/written work?

ROLE PLAY AS FUN – TEACHING HISTORICAL SKILLS

A second aspect of role play is using it to teach historical skills. Getting pupils to analyse sources and apply source skills consistently is one of the hardest tasks that a history teacher faces. For many, questions such as 'What does Source A tell us about . . .' or 'Why would the author of Source A have said this . . .' are incredibly boring and over a long period can put pupils off history. This is obviously a concern when many GCSE syllabuses still place a huge emphasis on source skills in their written papers. Role play can transform pupils' views of sources. Consider the following exercise:

Read Sources A and B.

 Why do these two sources give such different interpretations of the treatment of apprentices in nineteenth-century mills? Use the sources and your own knowledge to explain your answer.

Source A

A government official who was checking up on conditions for apprentices in mills after the 1833 Factory Act was told this about Quarry Bank Mill in 1835 by a local official. At this time the mill was a major local employer and the centre of the local economy bringing needed prosperity to the area of Styal, Cheshire:

On a sunny bank stands a handsome house, built for the accommodation of the female apprentices. Here, sixty young girls are well fed, clothed, educated and lodged. The female apprentices at Quarry Bank Mill come partly from its own parish, but chiefly from the Liverpool poor-house. Their ages vary from ten to twenty-one years.

 The apprentices have milk-porridge for breakfast, potatoes and bacon for dinner, and butcher-meat on Sundays. They have bacon every day.

(Factory Inspectors Report, H. C. (1835), p. xl)

Source B

In 1831–32 this is what one man told the Parliamentary enquiry into conditions in factories for children about his treatment some years earlier:

I was strapped most severely, till I could not bear to sit upon a chair without having pillows and I was forced to lie upon my face in the night time at one time. I was strapped both on my own legs and then I was put upon a man's back and then strapped. I was also buckled with two straps to an iron pillar, and flogged, all by one overlooker. After that he took a piece of rope, and twisted it in the shape of a cord, and put it in my mouth and tied it behind my head.

(Report on Employment of Children in Factories, H. C. 450 (1833), p. xx)

This question forms part of a mid-unit assessment on interpretations in a unit on the Industrial Revolution. Pupils have a good prior knowledge of its causes, and have studied the effects of industrialisation on health, factory conditions, and education. A conventional way to approach this question would be to discuss it in class, with pupils filling in a table looking at the five W's (who, what, why, where, when) and then completing the answer.

 Far more interesting is to 'act out' the sources:

1   Read through the sources – what do pupils notice? Dates? Language?
2   Either give two pupils pre-prepared cards of information or throw them in at the deep end. One is the poor man in Source B – s/he could be cross-examined either by the teacher or the pupils using intelligent and probing questions. Possible questions are:

* How can you remember details from so long ago?
* What did you think of your employer?
* How can we trust you?
* Are conditions still that bad?
* Why are you so angry?

Similarly for Source A:

- Why do you make out that conditions are so good?
- How can we trust you?
- Why are you so positive about the apprentices?

3   By eliciting answers to these questions, pupils are addressing the five W's and therefore giving themselves a good opportunity to answer the question. Responses could be completed on a simple chart that allows pupils to compare the two sources directly, and to seek out evidence of bias. Again, by emotionally engaging with the sources, pupils gain a greater understanding of sources and how to approach them.

This approach could be used for any source (see Activity 5.3) and any type of question on significance, interpretation or utility.

Activity 5.3   Role play and source work

Think of a lesson that is coming up which involves source work. How could you transform it using role play? Questions to consider:

- What will the source(s) be?

  _____

  _____

  _____

- Who will ask the questions – you or the class?

  _____

  _____

  _____

- What resources will you need to create?

  _____

  _____

  _____

- How will you assess what pupils have learnt – through oral understanding/a chart/written work?

  _____

  _____

  _____

- Did role play work better than a more conventional approach?

  _____

  _____

  _____

ROLE PLAY AS ASSESSMENT

Role play also offers a far more imaginative and enjoyable way to assess pupils' understanding of a historical topic. It is easy to become over-focused on a school marking policy that may grade work on an A1–D4 scale. Moreover, National Curriculum levels, important as they are, can dominate the assessment of pupils' work. Role play, however, can lead naturally to interesting forms of assessment, either without levels altogether or through self- or peer assessment, see Chapter 10 in this book.

One way in which this can be done is through a more demanding role play that assesses understanding of a unit. In Year 7, my department teaches aspects of the QCA unit on Islam, entitled 'Why were the Islamic Empires so successful between 600–1600?' It is an important unit that is also a Citizenship unit that addresses Citizenship Key Element 1d, about Britain as a diverse society. Within the unit, pupils learn about the teachings of Mohammed, the military success of early Islam, the wonders of Baghdad, achievements in architecture, the arts, mathematics, science, and Saladin and the Crusades. Rather than a written test or project, pupils are put into groups and given this task:

You are part of a local theatre company. You have two lessons to prepare and script a play that considers the question 'Why was Islam so successful between 600–1600?' Your group can use information in your exercise books, and any research that you can do outside of class. Your role play should be no more than 5 minutes long. You will be assessed by your teacher and the rest of the class on how well you can *explain* why Islam was so successful between 600–1600. Areas that you should cover are:

- the teachings of Mohammed;
- the military success of early Islam;
- the wonders of Baghdad;
- achievements in architecture, the arts, mathematics, science;
- Saladin and the Crusades.

This form of role play as assessment clearly needs a lot of planning and control. It should be treated as seriously as any other form of assessment. Guidance for successful management of a pupil-scripted role play includes:

1   Explain why pupils are doing this – each pupil is going to be assessed.
2   Be careful with group dynamics – who do you want working with each other?
3   Pupils must plan their ideas first – could one person be responsible for researching/ writing on a particular aspect of Islam?
4   Someone should be responsible for the script – the teacher could photocopy it later for each pupil.
5   Be clear on expectations – sensible behaviour, nothing silly, focus on the task.
6   Give pupils clear guidelines on timing – they need to get planning and writing straightaway. *Stick to the timings.*
7   Allow pupils to create props/costumes (if they wish) at home.
8   During the performance, get someone to time the role play and be firm on the timings.
9   A key part of role play like this is to get all pupils doing something – if pupils are assessing each other, then they could be filling in a sheet like the one below:

During each role play, tick the boxes if each group has covered that part of Islam. Give it a mark from 1 (Excellent) to 5 (Poor) according to how well explained each aspect is. Give some examples of how well they explained and then give the group a final score (out of 25).

Group	Mohammed	Military	Baghdad	Culture	Crusades	FINAL SCORE

By group assessing the activity, pupils can reflect on each other's work, and understand why some groups perhaps explained better than others. This will guarantee a debate about what makes a good explanation, which could then be tied to a written answer to the question. Alternatively, pupils could watch the role plays and then answer a self-assessment sheet on what they have learnt during the unit.

This activity could be extended elsewhere, and I have used it successfully in debates on 'Who caused World War I?' (Year 9), 'What should be done at Versailles?' (Years 9 and 10) and 'Who caused the Cuban Missile Crisis?' (Year 9). The key is pupils getting into role and really focusing on their level of explanation. There is also an excellent opportunity for pupils to use PowerPoint as a means of getting their points across.

Activity 5.4 has been designed for you to use role play as a means of assessing National Curriculum knowledge, skills and understanding. For this, select a unit of study from each of the Years 7 to 10 and, using the proforma, work out what Key Elements could be assessed.

ROLE PLAY AS DELIVERER OF KNOWLEDGE AND UNDERSTANDING

This final means of using role play, as a way of delivering knowledge and understanding, owes much to the revolutionary approach of Phil Smith, when he was at Coney Green High School, Bury. Smith's approach focuses on teacher-led role play, in short bursts, that engages all of the pupils in the classroom through vigorous questioning, getting pupils in to role and ensuring that all participate. Suitably energised, role play can lead to another activity, perhaps extended writing. It can be used as a one-off activity or, even better, throughout a unit, in order to really reinforce understanding.

One obvious advantage, again, is that this approach can stimulate pupils of all abilities. An excellent area to look at is Weimar Germany, between 1918–1933, in the GCSE Modern World syllabus. Phil Smith's approach is to look at the period by focusing on key events such as the Kaiser's abdication, Ebert and the Spartakists/Kapp Putsch, the signing of the Treaty of Versailles, hyperinflation and the occupation of the Ruhr. Pupils are chosen as the key figures, and are asked careful closed and open questions by the teacher about their situation – what will they do? Pace and motivation keep students interested, and help to provide a good understanding of the events covered, from all angles (Smith 2001; Smith 2002).

Activity 5.4 Role play as assessment

Use this grid to help you plan for assessment – you will need to use the History programme of study for this.
Tick off which skills will be assessed – how will the role play enable pupils to demonstrate their grasp of these skills?

Unit of work	Role play activity	Chronology KSU 1	Events/People/ Changes in the past KSU 2	Historical interpretation KSU 3	Historical enquiry KSU 4	Organisation and communication KSU 5	Form of assessment
		How will this skill be assessed?	Will the role play assess characteristic features/diversity/ causation/trends/ significance?	How will this skill be assessed?	How will this skill be assessed?	How will this skill be assessed?	

This approach works really well with areas at both Key Stage 3 and Key Stage 4 that are 'difficult to teach'. One example is the Year 8 module 'How important was the French Revolution 1789–1794?' The events between 1789–1793 are complex – by making one pupil Louis XVI, and giving s/he different problems to confront (Declaration of the Rights of Man, flight to Varennes, war with Austria, the September Massacres), pupils can understand how the Revolution radicalised after the storming of the Bastille. Better still, pupils could be put into groups (e.g. peasants, lawyers, urban workers, the aristocracy) and asked for their reaction to the events using prompt cards like the one below:

Peasants

You are still poor after the Revolution.
You are not sure if you still want a King.
You want the land to be shared out equally between everyone.

Again, this activity could lead anywhere, but pupils should be aware of why they are engaged in a task. Could you think of any areas of the history syllabus that would suit this style of teacher-led role play? Consider Activity 5.5.

Activity 5.5   Teacher-led role play

Think of an area (or areas) of the history curriculum that you feel you might find difficult to teach. How could a dynamic teacher-led role play transform your teaching? Questions to think about:

- What areas are difficult to teach – why are they difficult?
- How can my role play help clarify conceptual or other difficulties faced by pupils?
- Who will I involve in the role play?
- How can I ensure that all pupils are participating?
- What questions will I need to prepare?
- How will I maintain pace/excitement?
- How will I assess what pupils have learnt – question and answer/written work/self-assessment?

---

www

For further examples of the use of role play, see
http://www.routledge.com/textbooks/9780415370240

SUMMARY

Role play can revolutionise your teaching of history if you consider the following points:

- It should always be properly planned and fit naturally into a scheme of work – it is not a bolt-on extra.
- Pupils should be aware of what they are doing and why.

- There are different forms of role play – you need to decide which is most appropriate for what you are teaching.
- Role plays can enthuse pupils and thereby raise attainment of all pupils.
- Role plays can be used in innovative ways as a form of assessment.

As long as these principles are followed, be confident in how role play can improve your teaching and develop pupils' understanding.

FURTHER READING

In addition to the articles described in the chapter, you will find two further articles by Ian Luff extremely useful. They are:

Luff, I. (2000) 'I've been in the Reichstag: rethinking role play', *Teaching History*, 100.
Luff, I. (2003) 'Stretching the strait jacket of assessment: use of role play and practical demonstration to enrich pupil experience of history at GCSE and beyond', *Teaching History*, 113.

The September 2002 edition of *Teaching History* has a number of excellent resources, and most editions of *Teaching History* contain an example of role play in action

Chapter 6

Teaching causal reasoning

CHRISTOPHER CHAMBERS

INTRODUCTION

The aim of this chapter is to help trainee teachers plan lessons around the concept of causation, addressing key questions in relation to planning and teaching. Causation can be both the easiest and one of the most difficult historical skills to teach. If causation is seen merely as letting pupils know the reasons why an event took place, then teaching becomes relatively straightforward. The reasons are given to the pupils, who are then asked merely to comprehend and remember them; this is how the concept had traditionally been taught. However, if the aim is to engage the pupils in real historical thinking, it is altogether much more demanding. Teaching this concept is fraught with danger as misconceptions abound (see *Learning to Teach History in the Secondary School*, 2nd edn, Routledge, 2001, pp. 112–13).

Second-order concepts, such as causation and change, are central to history teaching and as such the former is a concept, which can be taught on many occasions. When looking at most events in history, it is likely that some time will be devoted to exploring why it happened. However, to teach the concept effectively, causation needs to be the focus of a series of lessons, not just one objective in part of a lesson. Often the topics, which can sustain this level of scrutiny, are the major events in history, such as wars or times of revolutionary change. These provide a complex web of causes, many of which can be traced back over many years prior to the event.

This chapter will focus on such a topic: the English Civil War. Reference will be made to a case study of three lessons; how those lessons were planned and taught will highlight issues, which need to addressed by a trainee teacher. The aim of the tasks and the worksheets is to reconsider the issues raised within the specific context of a school placement.

Chapter aims

By the end of the chapter you should be able to:

- identify those historical topics, which can best serve the teaching of causation;
- understand the range of learning objectives, which arise from exploring causation;
- employ possible approaches to stimulate pupils' initial interest in learning about causation;
- frame a good enquiry question, which will help pupils to be able to develop their causal reasoning;

- understand the reasons for providing the knowledge necessary for the development of pupils' causal reasoning and to use different approaches to provide this knowledge;
- consider the role of the teacher in helping pupils to develop their causal reasoning.

WHAT EXACTLY SHOULD PUPILS LEARN ABOUT CAUSATION?

Having identified which topic will provide the focus for an exploration of the concept (see Activity 6.1), it is crucial to consider which aspects of causation will be developed. To state in lesson plans that children are 'to develop their understanding of causation' is not at all helpful. There is a need for much more specific learning objectives.

Activity 6.1 KS3 topics

Look at the topics covered at a school during Key Stage 3. You might initially just want to look at those, which will be covered during the time you are on school experience.

Identify the topics that could lend themselves to developing causal reasoning in some depth.

Yet what exactly do we want the pupils to learn about causation? Discussions on this can be traced back to Carr (1961), whose thinking influenced the original National Curriculum (DES, 1991). This question has also exercised the minds of researchers (Lee *et al.*, 1995) and practitioners alike (Chapman, 2003). The importance of all this work is that it helps to clarify the type of lesson objectives associated with this concept.

Some possible objectives when teaching causation are:

- to appreciate and/or know there are reasons why the event happened;
- to highlight causes from a narrative account;
- to make links between causes;
- to organise the causes into categories (social, economic, political, religious, etc.);
- to distinguish between the long-term (trends) and short-term (triggers) causes of an event;
- to order causes into a hierarchy of importance.

A real danger for you as a trainee teacher is the desire to look at an historical skill from every angle. Attempting to cover too many aspects of causation with one topic can leave the pupils confused. Therefore, before planning lessons, it is worth finding out what the pupils have already done to develop their causal reasoning (Activity 6.2).

WHAT CAN BE LEARNT ABOUT CAUSATION FRON A CASE STUDY?

With the topic and objectives decided, the lessons can be planned. This raises another set of questions, which will be addressed by exploring a case study of three lessons on the Civil War in the seventeenth century taught to Year 8 pupils. It might be useful to download the lesson plans and resources before reading the rest of the chapter. The pupils had looked at causation on a number of occasions since Year 7, but this was the first time they would be exploring

Activity 6.2 Previous causal reasoning

For the classes where you will have the opportunity to teach causal reasoning, study the previous work of the pupils, and, if possible, talk to the class teacher. Look at the pupils' work and consider what skills they have already developed and to what extent they are secure in their grasp of that skill. What insights do you gain about the pupils' current understanding of the concept? Your lessons need to build on this, either by consolidating or developing the pupils' understanding further.

Can you now identify which objectives will be the focus for your lessons?

the concept in any depth. Thus the main objectives for these lessons were to enable the pupils to identify and classify reasons for the war.

www

For the lesson plans and teaching materials related to this chapter, see

http://www.routledge.com/textbooks/9780415370240

Where is the best place to start lessons on causation?

It is important to think about effective ways to introduce causation to pupils. In this case, the first lesson was critical as it needed to engage the pupils sufficiently to maintain their engagement for all three lessons. If this lesson is successful, it will hopefully generate momentum, which can be sustained. Phillips (2001) outlines a range of approaches to achieve this; ways in which teachers can make pupils curious and want to know more. One of these is the 'cut-off image' and it inspired the initial activity of the first lesson.

Pupils were presented with a Dutch print of the execution of Charles, but with the central scene blank. The image was laminated enabling the pupils to draw an outline of the missing scene. Although laminating is more expensive, it is cheaper in the long run as the resource can be reused by other classes. Of course, the children do not need to draw on the picture; the activity can be just as effective as a paired discussion. It might seem strange to start a sequence of lessons on the reasons for the civil war with an event from the end of the story. However, there is a clear principled justification for this approach. Just as not all detective fiction is about 'whodunnit', but how it happened, when teaching causation it is an effective strategy to begin with an event and then work back to explore why it took place. This approach is supported by practising teachers; for example, Clark (2001) argues that pupils need to see the consequences of a chain of events to help them to focus on what they will be asked to explain.

In order to complete this task, the pupils had to study the source and look for clues, which might help them to speculate as to what is happening in the picture. In addition, they will draw on their prior knowledge of the period. The key to the success of this phase was in keeping the questions open. In some schools, do not be surprised if there are pupils who are already familiar with this event; they can still be involved in the activity, as the purpose of the activity is to explore a visual source, rather than gain factual knowledge. Activity 6.3 will help you to clarify your ideas about stimulating pupils' curiosity.

Activity 6.3   Stimulating pupils' curiosity

1   Revisit the topics identified in Activity 6.1. Consider what might be effective Initial Stimulus Material, which will motivate the pupils to want to know the reasons why an event happened.
2   Discuss this with your mentor, and other staff in the department. How do they make pupils initially curious about these topics?
3   Read Phillips' (2001) 'Initial Stimulus Material', *Teaching History*, 105.
4   Complete this mind map in Figure 6.1.

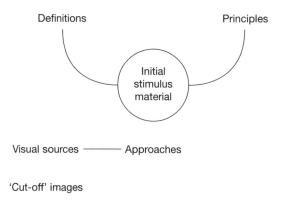

Figure 6.1 Mind map of initial stimulus material

What makes a good enquiry question?

The crucial purpose of the starter activity was to engage and interest pupils so that they *wanted* to know how this man came to be executed. The success of the starter was the fact it created a problem for the pupils to solve: why was it that a king, who normally was the person who gave the orders for someone to be executed, was himself the person about to be beheaded? Thus, the focus enquiry question for the pupils to address was 'Why did King Charles I lose his head?' A question, such as this, could encompass not just the causes of the war, but also Charles' actions during the war and his trial. In turn, it could lead to a useful assessment task at the end of this unit of study.

Clearly a question like 'Why did King Charles I lose his head?' cannot be answered in one lesson. This is 'the big question' which can be returned to periodically throughout the unit of work, most likely at the start and end of a lesson. However, each individual lesson will have a little question, which can be answered by the end of the lesson. In this first lesson, where the narrative only went up to 1629, it was 'Why did Charles and Parliament begin to fall out?' In the second lesson, the story was taken up to 1642.

These two key questions were not introduced to the pupils until half-way through the first lesson. There will be some schools, which insist on beginning each lesson with outlining the objectives beforehand. This approach does not always work for history, especially when the aim is to develop a sense of mystery. Of course, it is crucial that pupils have a clear sense of purpose to their learning, but there is no point in slavishly following school convention if it runs counter to the rationale for a lesson. Activity 6.4 will help you to clarify your thinking about the wording of the enquiry question.

Activity 6.4 Wording an enquiry question

Below is a list of questions that could be used to focus an enquiry around causal reasoning. Identify which would work best in the classroom by considering the wording of each question for its historical validity and its potential to engage pupils:

- What were the key events leading up to the Peasants' Revolt in 1381?

_____

_____

- 'There would have been no civil war if Charles I had avoided war with Scotland.'
  How far do you agree with this viewpoint?

_____

_____

- Is it possible to explain why Britain became the First Industrial Nation?

_____

_____

- What were the causes of the French Revolution?

_____

_____

- How important a factor was rebellion in persuading the British to end slavery in the Caribbean in 1833?

_____

_____

- Why did it take so much longer for British women to get the vote?

_____

_____

- How was it that, by 1900, Britain controlled nearly a quarter of the world?

_____

_____

- 'Hitler came to power largely because he was able to convince enough people that he had impressive individual qualities as a leader.'
  How far do you agree with this explanation of Hitler's rise to power in Germany?

_____

_____

Activity 6.4 *continued*

- Did the Treaty of Versailles cause the Second World War?

  _____

  _____

- How and why did the Holocaust happen?

  _____

  _____

What is the best way of providing the necessary historical knowledge?

One of the on-going tensions in teaching history is achieving the right balance between widening pupils' historical knowledge and developing their historical skills. Before any analysis of causation can take place, pupils need to be secure in their understanding of the narrative and so teachers need to establish a strong chronological factual base.

There are a number of ways in which the historical content can be covered: for example, a video or a role play, where events are introduced while pupils are in character. However, the most common is a written narrative, taken either from a textbook or an information sheet. The book with the perfect narrative has not been published, though some are clearly better than others. Choosing the right narrative to use can lead to agonising choices, which is often resolved by a trainee teacher producing their own information sheet. This can be very time-consuming and the danger is the focus of a trainee's energy has shifted from skills towards content.

In the case of the Civil War lessons, there are a range of textbooks. Some favour a straightforward narrative (Clare, 1997); others present the narrative in the form of dramatic dialogue (Byrom *et al.*, 1997). As the school did not possess suitable textbooks, the pupils were given teacher-produced resources, which were adapted from an Internet site (http://www.historylearningsite.co.uk/civil_war_england.htm).

One advantage of having resources in an electronic format is that it can help with differentiation. There were differences in the resources used by pupils in different sets. The more able pupils were provided with additional challenge, while the less able pupils required additional support, see Table 6.1.

When producing such resources, it is imperative to set a clear upper time limit as to how long will be spent on their production. It is worth remembering that the objective of these lessons was not for the pupils to know every event leading up to the war, but to appreciate how certain events led to a deterioration in relations between king and parliament (Activity 6.5).

Table 6.1 Differentiating resources

Support	Core	Challenge
Cards with seven key events with separate visual sources linked to each event.	A3 narrative sheet on events from 1625–1642 with four visual sources.	More detailed A3 narrative sheet, with two illustrations and extra information on King James I.

Activity 6.5 Finding suitable resources

Consider how the pupils will be provided with the necessary historical knowledge. Start by looking at how the topic is covered in a range of textbooks. If you find an approach which suits your purpose, you might base your lesson on that. If not, you will need to think about using the Internet. Remember to set a limit for how long you will spend searching for, and then adapting, resources.

Which teaching strategies match the learning objectives?

The teaching strategies will be dependent on the learning objectives; it is essential for there to be a clear link between the two. For the Civil War lessons, the main objectives were to enable the pupils to do the following:

1   identify possible causes for the breakdown in the relations between Charles and Parliament;
2   suggest possible ways of categorising the causes of the Civil War.

To achieve the first objective, the pupils were asked to re-read the text to highlight possible reasons. As the information was on a sheet, this could be done directly onto paper by underlining or highlighting phrases. This activity was partially successful in that the pupils were able to distinguish between factors which would, and would not, have led to a breakdown in relations; thus, they were able to appreciate the war was not due to Charles' lack of stature. However, the problem was that for many, they were unable to distinguish between the main point of a paragraph and the accompanying details and so too much text was highlighted. Although this is a common difficulty, it does not in itself reveal a lack of understanding of causation.

To achieve the second objective, the main strategy used was the card sort, which is probably the most common approach for teaching causation. This is where individual reasons for an event are written on separate sheets of paper and the pupils have to organise and classify them. Sometimes, the reasons are provided for the pupils already printed on card. In this case, the pupils would be writing onto paper the causes they have already highlighted. From there, it is easy for the pupils to move the cards to create patterns and orders. The success of the card sort revolves around the quality of the discussion as the pupils discuss possible links.

However, there can be a number of problems associated with card sorts and before using this strategy for the first time, it is worth thinking about the solutions to these. The distribution and collection of the cards present problems. It is a lot easier to manage if the cards are numbered and in envelopes.

Another problem comes when the pupils are to record the information from the cards once these have been sorted. Some schools like to see work in the pupils' exercise books and the danger can be that after the high level thinking associated with a card sort, the pupils spend the rest of the lesson on the low level task of simply copying the cards into their books. This should be avoided at all costs. It is better to ask the pupils to explain the cards in their own words, but depending on the number of cards, it can be difficult to sustain pupil concentration on the task. One alternative is to use glue pens to stick the cards onto paper or into their exercise books, though in addition there will need to be some task, either written or oral, to ascertain each pupil's engagement with the task.

A much more serious problem with card sorts is that pupils complete the task mechanistically. What can happen is they can scan for key words associated with a category without reading the whole of the card. This is a particular problem if the card sort has been divorced from the narrative. In some publications, the cards replace the narrative and it can be difficult for pupils to appreciate the chronology of the topic. In some respects, this approach is not dissimilar to the way causation was taught in the past when pupils were simply given a list of causes and told to memorise them. So, it is important to get the pupils to discuss why an event would have caused the Civil War. Activity 6.6 will help you to ensure there is a clear link between your objectives and the tasks you set.

Activity 6.6 Links between objectives and tasks

For each of the objectives, consider possible approaches you could take in the classroom. The key is to ensure that what the pupils will be doing matches what they should be learning.

Causation objective	Possible strategies
• to make links between causes	
• to organise the causes into categories (social, economic, political, religious, etc.)	
• to distinguish between the long-term (trends) and short-term (triggers) causes of an event	
• to order causes into a hierarchy of importance	

What will be the learning outcomes?

When planning, it is important to consider what the outcomes will be; that is, what the pupils will actually produce. So having decided on a card sort strategy, the next step is to decide what they will do once the cards have been sorted. The aim of categorising cards is to help pupils identify the underlining causes of an event. One of the key misconceptions that pupils have with causation is the confusion between events and causes; these can be interchangeable. This leads to the danger of pupils seeing causes simply as a list of events. The skill of a history teacher is to help pupils to realise that these events illustrate the underlying reasons for an event.

The most common classification for the Civil War is to identify the economic, political and religious causes of the conflict. This helps to consolidate that the underlying reasons for the war were disagreements about money, power and religion. The problem is certain events, like the war with Scotland, can be classified under more than one category. This can be overcome by asking the pupils to place their cards onto a Venn diagram (see below); this

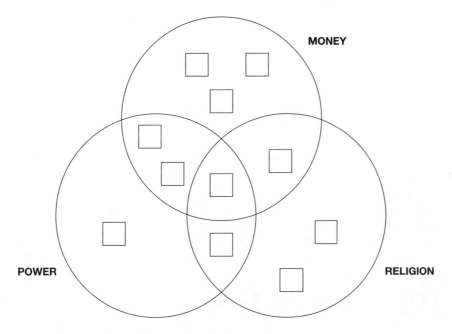

Figure 6.2 Venn diagram of underlying reasons for the war

brilliant idea first surfaced in *Changing Minds* (Byrom *et al.*, 1997). The Venn diagram in Figure 6.2 shows the overlap of money, power and religion.

If pupils have never categorised events before, it is worth initially giving them the headings beforehand. However, when this strategy is revisited, the pupils could have the opportunity to work on their own classifications. This can be another way of differentiating the task. In the case of the Civil War lessons, it was found that with very little prompting, nearly all pupils, irrespective of ability, were able to see that money was an issue. Some were also able to suggest the category of religion. Pupils did struggle at this point and some produced a 'catch-all' category like 'other'. Interestingly, some pupils selected an event (e.g. Charles' marriage) as a category in itself, which demonstrates they are not as secure in their understanding.

Some trainees, like the pupils, feel it is important to have the 'right answer' on paper but the danger can be that to achieve this so much teacher help is required that the whole class has exactly the same response to the task. This is not at all helpful when it comes to assessing pupils' understanding of the concept. It is crucial for trainee teachers to resist the temptation to provide the right answer. The key here is not to worry if pupils make errors; these mistakes will help to consider the next steps to be taken when this concept is revisited. One measure of progress in causation is to apply causal reasoning to a different context.

Once the diagram has been completed, there are a number of possible outcomes. The most obvious is to produce a piece of extended writing with the categories becoming potential paragraphs. However, it is possible that the pupils could be working towards a debate or a presentation, or producing a newspaper or pamphlet from one side or the other (Activity 6.7). Whatever the outcome, the key is to ensure it is consistent with your objective.

Activity 6.7 Final outcome

Consider what you want the pupils to produce. This does not necessarily have to be a written task, but if it is, think about what type of writing you want to develop. You might consider alternatives, where there is an oral outcome.

What is the role of the teacher during causation lessons?

From research carried out to establish how pupils make progress in history (Lee *et al.*, 1995), one key finding that emerged is that pupils' responses tend to be task specific. Thus, when teaching causal reasoning, pupils might do well with one task on one topic but then perform poorly when revisiting the skill in a different context. This is an important conclusion. Simply providing pupils with an opportunity to study causation does not necessarily lead to a consequent development of causal reasoning. Teaching any historical skill is not simply about producing resources and assuming that in doing their work, the pupils will develop understanding. You need to think about how teachers can help their pupils develop their causal reasoning. Through their skills of explanation and exposition, teachers can aid pupils' understanding. When teaching causation, simple visual aids and analogies can assist in this process (Activity 6.8). For example, when trying to explain how certain events can be triggers, the use of the children's game *Buckaroo*, or blowing up a balloon until it bursts, can be very effective props. It is always worth remembering that teachers really do make a difference and it is the lesson where the teacher does something different, which is remembered.

Activity 6.8   Teaching causation

Log on to the following website: http://www.historyitt.org.uk Follow the links to Unit 6.2.2. This section explores debates about the nature of history and contains a number of excellent activities, which will help to develop, and clarify, your thinking about teaching causation.

SUMMARY

This chapter has considered the main questions, which need to be addressed when planning lessons around the concept of causation. Emerging from the chapter are four key principles, which should inform this process:

1   It is important to have *clear and specific objectives*, which consolidate and develop the pupils' understanding of the concept.
2   *It is crucial to engage the pupils fully* so that they genuinely want to understand why an event occurred. The use of initial stimulus material and a challenging enquiry question are two ways suggested in the chapter to achieve this.
3   It is essential to *achieve the right balance* between providing background historical knowledge and developing the skills.
4   *The activities devised must be consistent with the objectives and should allow the pupils to think independently.* It is important as a teacher to avoid the temptation to direct the pupils towards the 'right answer'.

ACKNOWLEDGEMENT

The author expresses his gratitude to Sharon Ashworth, Sarah Cheshire, Louise Taberner, and the Year 8 pupils at Fearns Community Sports College in Lancashire, for their assistance in the teaching and evaluation of, and responses to, these lessons on the Civil War.

FURTHER READING

Scott, J. (1990), *Understanding Cause and Effect*, London: Longman.

Chapter 7　Teaching historical interpretations

YVONNE SINCLAIR

INTRODUCTION

The place and development of historical interpretations in the curriculum have been succinctly described by Davies and Williams (1998) and teachers' thinking about its teaching and learning has been influenced by the work of McAleavy (2000). Through studying interpretations pupils begin to understand the nature of history, how it is created and how history works. Pupils can learn that there is not just one version of the past, and that history can be used for propaganda purposes, too. In-depth study of historical controversies and mysteries are encouraged and allow the past to be considered from a range of perspectives. Historical interpretations enable 'lesser known histories' to be examined and allow questions about gaps and omissions in historical accounts to be asked, and this potential for an 'inclusive history' continues to be explored (Wren, 1999, 2002; Grosvenor, 2000). An intellectually demanding concept, asking questions about interpretations, it helps pupils develop higher-order cognitive skills.

Yet, in spite of these attributes, the teaching of this concept continues to present a real challenge to teachers and in particular to trainee history teachers. It is notable that many of the excellent texts published in recent years for pupils at KS3 have paid significantly less attention to this concept than to other second-order concepts and skills and in *History in Secondary Schools* (2001) Ofsted reported that 'knowledge and understanding of historical interpretations are the weakest elements of learning in history'.

Yet, while historical interpretations are subject to much discussion, a great deal of innovative and exciting classroom practice is taking place. Teachers have taken advantage of the fact that interpretations and representations of historical events, people and issues occur in such a wide variety of media. Lessons have been embellished by the use of film, historical fiction, paintings and poetry. The journal *Teaching History* has become an important forum for the sharing of practice and a relevant and important recent development has been its feature 'Polychronicon', which discusses 'recent historiography and changing interpretation'.

The aim of this chapter is to help you consider and address some of the challenges facing both pupils and teachers when teaching this Key Element. It discusses a series of lessons given to a Year 8 group on the Industrial Revolution, highlighting key issues to help you with your own planning and teaching of this concept.

Chapter aims

By the end of this chapter you should be able to:

- research and plan a topic for the teaching and learning of historical interpretations;
- make use of the range of objectives available for the study of historical interpretations;
- understand the preconditions in terms of pupils' knowledge and understanding for successful lessons on historical interpretations;
- establish criteria for the selection of sources for the teaching and learning of historical interpretations;
- devise a series of activities in which pupils assess and evaluate historical interpretations.

PREPARING TO TEACH ABOUT HISTORICAL INTERPRETATIONS

Choosing a topic

It is probably the inclusion of interpretations in the curriculum that has encouraged teachers to engage pupils in enquiries that ask them to consider different versions of the past (Activity 7.1). Interpretative questions such as 'Cromwell: Hero or Villain?' have become quite popular. Such questions give pupils an opportunity to explore real historical controversies and, when explored in depth, pupils can begin to develop their understanding of historical interpretations, preparing the way for evaluation of historical accounts based on pupils' own subject knowledge.

Activity 7.1 Analysis of textbooks and GCSE papers

1   Take three history texts produced for use by pupils at Key Stage 3 and focus on one of the three British units of study.
2   What questions are being asked about historical interpretations? What types of historical interpretations are being examined? How? What types of activities are being set for pupils? What use is being made of sources of evidence?
3   Perform a similar task with a selection of GCSE papers set over the last five years.

The key question 'Was the Industrial Revolution good or bad for the people of Britain?' offers a good opportunity to develop pupils' understanding of historical interpretations as well as providing an opportunity to consider 'historical writings'. This type of historical interpretation has been less well exploited than other more glamorous and often more accessible types of interpretations such as film and other visual portrayals of the past. Use of historians' writings can prove difficult for the beginning teacher.

Pupils' background knowledge and prior learning

One of the first things you need to be aware of is context. In particular you need to know as much as possible about the pupils you will be teaching. What is their level of ability? How good are their literacy skills? And before you can expect pupils to evaluate a particular interpretation you need to ensure that they have sufficient knowledge and understanding of key aspects of the topic under scrutiny.

> **WWW**
>
> For the details of the sources and the interpretations used, the lesson plans, and support material for the worksheets, see
>
> http://www.routledge.com/textbooks/9780415370240

The class I worked with was a top ability Year 8 group. The pupils had already studied in some depth key aspects of the Industrial Revolution: its causes, the mills, the workers; inventions; the coal industry and its dangers; health, disease and urbanisation. There had been some significant emphasis upon child labour and pupils had briefly considered how people's lives had changed. They had used a range of sources to carry out their enquiries and to develop their subject knowledge. Their work had clearly been influenced by the popular text *Minds and Machines* (Byrom *et al.*, 1999) and key questions about the nature of sources of evidence had been addressed. Study of different contemporary explanatory accounts and viewpoints of the Peterloo Massacre had also given them some awareness of different versions and interpretations of past events. Thus the pupils, even to a greater extent than the Year 7 class studying interpretations described in Chapter 3, had:

- good prior subject content knowledge;
- useful evidential skills;
- some initial understanding of historical interpretations.

For my four lessons I could build upon this.

The learning objectives

There are many objectives that relate to the teaching and learning of interpretations (there is a detailed list of these on the website). You are more likely to be successful if you restrict any lesson to just one or two specific objectives (Activity 7.5). The aim here was to begin to develop the pupils' ability to understand, assess and evaluate a particular interpretation using 'criteria of congruence with facts, comprehensiveness and consistency' (Lee, and Shemilt, 2004, p. 26). I wanted pupils to understand that:

> **Activity 7.2 Pupil misconceptions**
>
> Ask your mentor or Head of Department to select a small group of four or five pupils for a (tape) discussion. Select four varied interpretations related to a topic they have recently studied, e.g. a picture, a contemporary source, an extract from a Key Stage 2 book and a modern author. Consider what questions you could ask the group which would address the following misconceptions. These are:
>
> (i)   that interpretations that are written have greater legitimacy than those in other media.
> (ii) that the interpretation of an eye-witness is more likely to be the truth than that of a non-contemporary view.

interpretations really can be tested and confirmed or falsified by an appeal to the evidence; and some of the time at least, it really is possible to prove that one side is right and one side is wrong. What counts as evidence is not determined solely by one historian's perspective, but is subject to a wide measure of agreement which transcends the individual.

(Evans, 1997, p. 128)

Thus the principal learning objective for this series of lessons was for pupils to *assess and evaluate a particular historical interpretation*. The interpretation was to be tested against pupils' own subject knowledge and their understanding of the evidence, and would allow the pupils to appreciate the process whereby an interpretation came into existence.

You will often find that your principal objective will need to be broken down further, providing a logical sequence to your series of lessons. The pupils were to do the following:

1   understand how accounts are related to particular questions asked by the author (and are thus necessarily selective);
2   understand how sources of evidence are at the basis of interpretations;
3   understand how sources can be used to substantiate or discredit particular interpretations;
4   use subject knowledge and evidence to evaluate the 'worth' and validity of a particular account;
5   create their own interpretations and thus begin to appreciate the legitimacy of different interpretations.

Selecting relevant and appropriate sources

This is probably the area requiring most attention when you are planning to teach about interpretations and, as such, this is given particular attention here. Sources and accounts need to be selected carefully and with the specific learning objectives in mind. Yet it is a process that has its own intrinsic interest.

Sources for Lesson One

The criteria for choice of sources was that they should:

1   be contemporary and mostly primary sources to contrast to the historian's accounts;
2   be varied, with a range of impressions and viewpoints to show pupils how sources are a basis for interpretations and how they can be used to support or discredit interpretations. Therefore, included were visual sources, petitions, personal recollections, tables, interviews, adverts, speeches, and the websites used;
3   be limited in number so as not to overwhelm the pupils. As small a number as is sufficient for the purpose.
4   include some sources the pupils had already met before.

Although there is ample coverage of the topic in textbooks, you will find it useful to seek electronic sources. Three examples that you may find especially relevant for the study of the Industrial Revolution are:

http://www.fordham.edu/halsall/
http://www.spartacus.schoolnet.co.uk/Irchild.main.htm
http://www.learningcurve.pro.gov.uk

These sites and others offer plenty of contemporary sources.

Sources for Lessons Two and Three

The choice of an interpretation for analysis and evaluation was particularly important for addressing the principal learning objective of this series of lessons. I selected an historian's account that was useful for pupil evaluation. An account by Lawrence Reed (2001) seemed most fit for purpose:

- It clearly and forcibly adopted a particular viewpoint. This is of great importance when you are initially trying to develop pupils' understanding of interpretations.
- It referenced and made use of primary and secondary sources of evidence, in support of its argument.
- It had a particular focus on the issue of 'child labour'. Thus, the amount of working subject knowledge pupils would need to help them in their assessment of a challenging written historical interpretation could be kept to a minimum.

The challenge was to make the Reed interpretation in particular accessible without distorting its content. There was some reduction in length; some words were substituted; and some of the complexities of the argument were removed. In addition, with colour coding of text, numbering of paragraphs, use of a glossary and, in lessons, significant use of teacher intervention in very structured tasks, changes could be kept to a minimum. Croft (2005) argues that working with challenging accounts written by real historians can be motivating and rewarding for the more able pupil. Croft also details how the use of structured tasks with Year 8 pupils can help them use a real historian's account to address a real historical question. You will often find yourself surprised by what pupils can do.

Sources for Lesson Four

For comparative purposes, a similarly partisan historian's account (by E.P. Thompson) was introduced to pupils, particularly relevant as it made use of some of the same sources used by Reed. Sources given in previous lessons were also used.

Now try Activity 7.3.

THE EXEMPLAR LESSONS

Organising pupils for learning and lesson structure is a key area for consideration prior to any lesson and is covered by the lesson descriptions and discussions below. The following four lessons target an able Year 8 or Year 9 class.

Lesson One: Sources as basis for interpretations

Key questions are: 'Was the Industrial Revolution good or bad for the people? What do the sources of evidence suggest?'

Starter

Pupils presented with five different visual images and, first in pairs and then as a whole class, discuss the question: 'Does the picture source give a positive or negative impression or viewpoint of the impact of the Industrial Revolution?'

Phase 2

- Pupils work in groups with a set of 12 laminated source cards (written, statistical and visual).
- Starter question repeated.

Activity 7.3 Researching and planning a topic for the teaching and learning of historical interpretations

Using the discussion in the chapter, the proforma below can be used in several ways: retrospectively applied to a lesson or lessons already observed; with other trainees working in pairs as a hypothetical exercise which could be used later or for a trainee planning for teaching.

1 Topic

2 Research. Sources of Interpretations
 	
Written (academic):
 	
    Literature:
 	
    Pictorial:
 	
    Film:
 	
    Buildings, statues:
 	
    Other:

3 Checklist of Interpretations
 	
Range and number of viewpoints:
 	
    Spread over time:
 	
    Accessibility:

4 Objectives You may find it useful to use the outcomes list on the website.
5 Methodology How will the pupils acquire the basic topic content? How will the interpretations be presented to the pupils? Organisation of pupils? Sequencing of tasks? What are the written learning outcomes?
6 Assessment How will you know whether the pupils have met the learning objectives?

- Pupils share the reading tasks and arrange sources into two or three piles, according to whether the sources would support a positive, negative or an ambivalent interpretation of the Industrial Revolution.
- Brief whole class feedback on pupil decisions.
- Pupils individually record their ideas in table form (see Table 7.1), completing the first three columns.

Table 7.1 Assessment of sources

Source	What does the source show?	Does it give a positive or negative or mixed impression or viewpoint of the impact of the Industrial Revolution?	Is there a reason why you may not be able to trust this source completely? Consider both its content and the author. Explain
A			
B			

Continued below for 12 sources

Phase 3

Pupils consider the reliability of the sources as sources of evidence for the question. Complete last column of Table 7.1.

Plenary

Teacher-led class discussion asking pupils: 'Do the sources suggest the Industrial Revolution was a good or a bad thing?' and 'What is their own viewpoint or opinion?' Pupils draw conclusions using prior subject knowledge and today's lesson. Pupils individually record their own responses for future reference.

In this lesson the pupils are being asked to use the content of the sources to make inferences about the 'viewpoint'/impression(s) the sources give about the impact of the Industrial Revolution. The question about reliability of source will be useful to pupils when they come to evaluate a particular interpretation and to develop their own interpretations. It is important for the teacher to begin the discussion about reliability before asking pupils to complete the fourth column of the table.

The teaching and learning approaches emphasise co-operative learning, with opportunities for pupil talk, sharing of ideas and thinking ideas through. The class was already familiar with group work. The teacher's role is primarily that of facilitator here, important for introducing tasks and reinforcing the key learning points.

By the end of this first lesson pupils begin to realise that a range of answers is likely to be possible to the question, 'Was the Industrial Revolution a good or a bad thing?'

Lesson Two: Analysing an historical interpretation

Key questions are: 'Was the Industrial Revolution a good or a bad thing (for children)? What is the interpretation of one historian?'

Starter

Using two contrasting sources from Lesson One, teacher reinforces and recaps points made at the end of previous lesson.

Phase 2

Unmarked copy of Lawrence Reed's interpretation distributed to each pupil. Pupils complete a series of structured and time-limited tasks (whole class, pair and individual work).

Each task is followed by class discussion with pupils being asked:

- whether Reed thinks the Industrial Revolution was bad or good?
- to use a marker to highlight words, phrases or sentences, which support their conclusions;
- to enumerate and highlight types of sources Reed uses as the basis for his argument, and those he dismisses.

Plenary

Teacher-led discussion and reinforcement of the main teaching points, i.e. an interpretation expresses a viewpoint, relates to a question asked and is based on sources of evidence and Reed argues that . . .

Together with Lesson Three, this lesson focuses on one historian's interpretation of an aspect of the impact of the Industrial Revolution. It begins the in-depth analysis and evaluation of Reed's account by attempting, first, to ensure that the pupils understand the argument presented and, second, to show how Reed uses sources to construct his case. With such a challenging written account, there is a strong emphasis on comprehension in the tasks set, and teacher input and questioning are of particular importance in developing and checking pupils' understanding. With the need for particularly close attention to text, pupil-to-pupil learning has been limited to pair work.

Lesson Three Evaluation and assessment of an historian's interpretation

Key questions are: 'Was the Industrial Revolution a good or a bad thing? What is the worth and validity of one historian's account?'

Starter

Recap on previous two lessons and their main teaching points.

Phase 2

- Continued detailed analysis and evaluation of the Reed interpretation.
- As before, unmarked copy of the account for each pupil.
- The pupils will undertake series of time-limited tasks, each followed by class discussion.
- In pairs and using their exercise books to summarise their decisions, the pupils will be asked to:

  - Re-visit the sources used by Reed and decide which ones really helped to make his argument.
  - Indicate which of their own sources do or do not support Reed, and which might contradict him.
  - Use their own knowledge and the sources to judge the 'worth' of Reed's interpretation and to decide whether or not they agree with him. Give reasons for opinions.

Plenary

Full class discussion of pupils' responses with answers with teacher summarising what the pupils have learned about the nature of historical interpretations; how interpretations are constructed; and how assessments and evaluations can be made of interpretations using given criteria. Pupils again are asked whether in their opinion the Industrial Revolution was a good or bad thing. In this lesson it is important that all the tasks set and questions asked help pupils to assess the worth and validity of Reed's interpretation. Now try Activity 7.4.

Activity 7.4 Asking questions of historical interpretations

1   Access the Thompson interpretation from the exemplar material on the chapter's website.
2   Devise a range of tasks which abler students in pairs could attempt with their copy of this extract to do the following:

    (i)   separate fact from opinion;
    (ii) note the extent to which the views are supported by evidence;
    (iii) consider whether the extract supports their views of the use of child labour;

3   Consider how you could make this historian's account accessible to a wider range of students.

Lesson Four Consolidating pupils' learning and the legitimacy of different accounts

Key questions are: 'Was the Industrial Revolution a good or a bad thing?' What do the pupils think? It has been recognized that 'students' own interpretations can be a useful way of introducing more general ideas about interpretations (McAleavy, 2000, p. 76) and in this last lesson, through writing their own answers to the question about the impact of the Industrial Revolution, it is hoped that the learning of the previous lessons will be consolidated.

Before setting the main task, pupils will be introduced to an interpretation in complete contrast to the earlier one (care will be needed to ensure the intended learning objectives remain in focus). Research into pupils' understanding of history has suggested that pupils begin by wanting 'one proper account' (Lee and Shemilt, 2004). I wanted pupils to understand the legitimacy of different interpretations, that there was nothing 'sinister' about the existence of different interpretations. I wanted them to understand that it was okay for them to draw different conclusions from their peers and, indeed, from Reed. In addition, this second account reinforces the notion that interpretations are based upon sources, thus E.P. Thompson has a key role to play in helping pupils become confident interpreters of the impact of the Industrial Revolution.

Starter

Teacher introduces aim and focus of the lesson, making clear links with the learning of the previous two lessons.

Phase 2

- Teacher reads an alternative interpretation of the question (E.P. Thompson extract), adopting changes of tone and volume for emphasis.
- Pupils receive a copy of the text and highlight the sources used by Thompson to support his case.
- In class discussion pupils begin to indicate how it differs from Reed.

Phase 3

Teacher introduces focus and task of remainder of lesson. Sources used in previous lessons made available to pupils. Teacher indicates procedure pupils might follow when writing interpretations: the choice of sources; use of the own knowledge from previous lessons; how to set out their piece of writing, making a plan, use of writing frames, etc.

Phase 4

Pupils given a minimum of 30 minutes to write interpretations.

Plenary

Teacher-led discussion of pupils' conclusions, including which sources of evidence and facts are used or dismissed by them. Main teaching points stressed once again.

As indicated in Phase 3, pupils will need careful guidance to help them develop and structure their work. Alternative approaches to extended writing could be adopted here, and indeed, after the structured work of Lessons Three and Four an approach allowing for fuller use of imagination and creativity might be a preferred choice, e.g. in groups, pupils could be asked to develop and present their own conclusions and viewpoint of the question in the form of *a display*. Captions to the sources or written commentary would need to be included to explain the viewpoints adopted.

Throughout this series of lessons you will have noted time allocated for reinforcement of learning, especially at the beginning and end of lessons. It is important that you always allow sufficient time for this, ensuring pupils are clear what they have learnt and are learning before moving on to the next activity. This will be of real importance here in the last lesson of the sequence, when the links between each of the lessons need to be made explicit.

> **www** For further ideas and materials to explain the differences between interpretations,
> see http://www.routledge.com/textbooks/9780415370240

The aim of Activity 7.5 is to help you to have a fuller understanding of the range of objectives for the learning of historical interpretations, to consider how they may be exemplified and taught.

Activity 7.5 Using the objectives

On the website associated with the chapter you will find a lengthy list of objectives for the learning of historical interpretations. They are divided into categories: range and variety; validity and worth; explanation of differences; definition and pupil interpretations.

Activity 7.5 *continued*

1 Read the description of the lessons on interpretations of the Industrial Revolution in the chapter and then consider whether objectives listed on p. 62 are addressed during the lessons described in the chapter and, if so, where.

2 Are there any other objectives in this list likely to have been met in the course of these lessons? If so, what lessons can be learned from this?

3 To develop further your understanding of this Key Element, take each of the objectives in the list in turn and suggest examples of interpretations you could use which would help a class achieve that objective.

4 Again using the list, in turn, consider the variety of pupil activities you could use which would lend themselves to the achievement of the objectives.

SUMMARY

Many trainee teachers regard historical interpretations as one of the most difficult aspects of teaching history. Success is more likely if:

- you ensure the pupils have sufficient grounding in the knowledge of the topic upon which the interpretations are based;
- there is a narrow focus for your choice of objectives from the considerable range related to the teaching of historical interpretations;
- both contemporary sources and secondary material are used to develop pupils' understanding;
- pupils' own enquiries have a key role to play in pupils' learning.

The focus of the pupils' evaluation in this chapter was upon an historian's interpretation. However, from your reading and observations you will soon appreciate and begin to explore the many varied and interesting media that can be used for such lessons. This will be particularly important when helping pupils to explain differences between the interpretations too. You will soon recognise that pupils' understanding of interpretations develops over time and that as a teacher it is your responsibility to look for opportunities within the curriculum to ensure this. As your own knowledge and understanding of learning objectives for historical interpretations develops, you will find teaching historical interpretations a challenging but a most rewarding aspect of your teaching.

ACKNOWLEDGEMENT

I would like to express thanks to Ryder Hargreaves, his department and the boys at Burnage High for Boys, Manchester, for their help.

FURTHER READING

Card, J. (2004) 'Seeing double: how one period visualizes another', *Teaching History*, 117.

Haydn, T., Arthur, J. and Hunt, M. (2001) *Learning to Teach History in the Secondary School*, London: Routledge, Chapter 6.

Lee, P. (1998) '"A lot of guess work goes on" children's understanding of historical accounts', *Teaching History*, 92.

Chapter 8 Ensuring inclusion in the classroom

ALISON STEPHEN

INTRODUCTION

As history teachers in the present educational climate, we face a huge and increasing challenge. Our aim is to make the subject accessible and enjoyable to pupils from diverse backgrounds, while proving to senior managers and government that history remains an essential part of the curriculum. At Key Stage 4 we are often competing against vocational courses, or more practical subjects in which it is easier for less academic students to attain the critical grades A* to C. We need therefore to make history popular with students and also to show its contribution in areas such as literacy, thinking skills and citizenship.

The demands of our subject are very high. We ask pupils not only to develop a whole set of subject-specific skills, but we require them to apply them to different historical topics, and to retain knowledge of these various topics. Success is measured in forms that require high levels of written English.

In our secondary schools, you will meet a wide variety of pupils with diverse learning needs. The reduction of places in special schools and the policy of inclusion in mainstream schools has meant a greater range of needs in our classrooms. These pupils include SEN; the very able; Speakers of English as an Additional Language (EAL), including asylum seekers and refugees, who are likely to have extra emotional and social needs; and pupils with different preferred learning styles (auditory, visual, kinaesthetic) (see *Learning to Teach History in the Secondary School*, 2nd edn, Routledge, 2001, pp. 167–70, for details of the needs of pupils with SEN or who are very able). The aim here is to outline some approaches that may help you to meet these needs, and help you learn how to adapt resources.

Chapter aims

By the end of this chapter you should be able to:

- understand how pictures can be used in a number of different ways as a focus for learning for all pupils;
- assess the advantages and disadvantages of different methods of differentiation;
- provide support for less able pupils in a range of different ways;
- identify the characteristics of very able pupils and understand how to address their learning needs;
- consider the needs of learners of English as an additional language and identify some ways of including them in learning.

COMMON STARTING POINTS

With a mixed ability class it is useful to begin a lesson with a common starting point. A brief starter activity can engage all pupils in learning and get them settled quickly. It can also lead to lots of useful discussion or source analysis. A picture used as initial stimulus can have meaning for all pupils, including the less able and those with EAL. Gifted pupils will ask questions of the pictures, and draw out more information. There is an obvious appeal to visual learners. Those who prefer to learn visually will need help to build up a picture of historical events, which are very unfamiliar to their mental framework.

You can also adapt these activities for kinaesthetic learners. Reading and writing, although intrinsic to the study of history, can have little appeal to kinaesthetic learners, who can lose interest and behave badly when not actively involved. To counteract this, try to get your pupils involved in physical activities as far as possible, e.g. card sorts, handling artefacts, acting out events, moving around the room, and so on. This is often best done at the start of the lesson as a hook for the development phase. The activities at the end of Table 8.1 are designed for kinaesthetic learners. The others can be adapted.

Table 8.1 Examples of starters using pictures

Activities	Purpose/when to use	Examples
1 Deduce what a picture is You could cover up part of it, and reveal a little at a time.	To introduce a new topic. Maybe an image that will appear strange to pupils.	• a photograph of a victim of shell shock receiving electric shock treatment after the First World War • Artefacts associated with the transatlantic slave trade, e.g. a punishment collar.
2 Think of words to describe the scene or the feelings of the people in it.	Work on attitudes (KSU 2a)	War scenes.
3 Compare two pictures.	To show change over time	• Two maps of the local area. • Pictures showing the inside of a Catholic and a Protestant church.
4 Label a picture or a cartoon.	Source analysis or to introduce a new topic	Street scene from a city in the early nineteenth century[1]
5 Memory tests – show a picture then hide it. Ask them to draw or write down as much as they remember. Can be done as group work.	Thinking skills, memory	Outline of a motte and bailey castle.
6 Pupils work in groups using different sets of pictures. Groups then compare notes to build up an overall picture.	Thinking skills – connections between pictures. Helps cover a lot of content quickly	• Scenes from the siege of Leningrad • Pictures from the Imperial War Museum pack on the role of black people in the First World War[2]
7 Place pictures around the room, and ask pupils to find a picture that shows . . .	Immediate involvement, and close study of sources	• Medieval village life • Machines from the Industrial Revolution.
8 Photocopy or paste a picture onto card, cut it up, place pieces in an envelope, and ask pupils to piece it together	Close study of a source	• Anti-Catholic propaganda engravings from the time of the Reformation[3]

Table 8.1 continued

Activities	Purpose/when to use	Examples
like a jigsaw. Eight pieces seems to be suitable for most pupils for an A4-sized picture. You could differentiate the task by producing some envelopes with fewer pieces and some with more.		
9 Require pupils to kiss or bow down to a picture of a leader.	To simulate a totalitarian regime.	Picture of Lenin
10 Sequence pictures – either sets of pictures on the desk, or one per pupil, so that they have to form a line.	Chronology – could lead to writing a narrative. To think about relative importance of events or ideas	• Life of Thomas Becket • Anti-Semitic measures in Nazi Germany
11 Sort pictures to decide which ones support certain hypotheses.	Classifying and making judgements	Home Front in WW2 – Was there a 'Blitz Spirit'?
12 Acting out a picture either by a small group, or by the whole class	To help pupils understand a situation	• Picture of the execution of Charles I[4] • Picture of medieval peasants at work • Picture of slaves crammed into a ship

Notes:
1 See website 'A Court for King Cholera', *Punch* cartoon, 1852. This cartoon, frequently used in textbooks, may be seen at several sites. Use Google Images then cartoon title.
2 Imperial War Museum pack – 'The Empire needs Men' – ISBN 1–870423–47X.
3 See picture and explanatory notes on chapter website.
4 See picture on website. The picture may be seen at http://www.en.wikipedia.org/wicki/Charles-I-of-England.

You can either find pictures from textbooks or by using an image search on a search engine. Your picture can be displayed on an interactive whiteboard or an OHT. Use of textbooks takes more time. Print copies if you want pupils to label or mark the picture. Answers are best made quickly in rough at the back of books, or on mini white boards. Try to reduce class question and answer sessions that allow many pupils to switch off. Give a time target to help pupils focus quickly.

Before using your starter activity with the class, you should think about the following:

- What resources need to be given out?
- Do pupils need to write anything down? If so, where? If writing in their books, they may expect to have to put a full title and date. Will this defeat the object of a quick start?
- Can you extend this task for the more able?
- Can latecomers get involved easily?
- How does the starter fit in with the rest of your lesson, and how will you explain this?
- How long do you expect it to take?

These examples can be adapted in many ways, and once you begin to use this type of task, you will begin to see the possibilities. Most of these tasks could also be done with artefacts or written sources. Many of the examples suggested are primary sources, simply because these tasks are a good way of introducing a primary picture source, which may appear strange to the untrained eye, and the detail and context of which could be missed if it is only given a quick glance (Activity 8.1). Detailed pictures may best be used for an activity such as a jigsaw, where close observation is required to complete the task.

Activity 8.1

1   Look at the picture of the execution of Charles I in note 4 Table 8.1. Think of three ways to use the picture. Include some more difficult questions or tasks to extend the more able.
2   Find a picture from one of the topics you will be teaching which could be cut up to make a jigsaw. Design some questions for discussion once the pupils have completed the jigsaw.
3   Look at the first activity in Table 8.1, and consider how to adapt it for kinaesthetic learners.

---

www

For detailed examples of the approaches mentioned in the text, see

http://www.routledge.com/textbooks/9780415370240

For Activity 8.2, you will need to acquire several textbooks and/or topic books used by the history department to which you are attached. Select those pictures you think you could use to exemplify each of the twelve activities listed in Activity 8.2. This could also be tackled as pair/group activity, when trainees could discuss their choices and how they would use the picture starters.

Activity 8.2   Matching pictures to starter activities

Using a variety of textbooks and topic books, find suitable pictures for the activities.

	Activity	Suitable pictures
1	Deducing what a picture says	
2	Think of words to describe the scene or people's feelings	
3	Comparing two pictures	
4	Labelling a picture	

Activity 8.2 *continued*

5	Memory tests	
6	Group work – different sets of pictures; comparison and overall picture	
7	Pictures around the room which show . . .	
8	Jigsaw activity, which would allow for differentiation	
9	Picture stimulating action, e.g. bowing	
10	Sequencing picture, e.g. chronologically	
11	Sorting pictures to support a hypothesis	
12	Acting out a picture/cartoon	

DIFFERENTIATION

Matching work to ability is crucial in order to engage all of your pupils and to aid classroom management. It may be necessary to differentiate work for a class that is banded or setted, as well as for a mixed ability group. In some cases, all pupils can access the same materials, given different levels of intervention by the teacher or classroom assistant. If you succeed in capturing your pupils' imagination at the start of the lesson, perhaps using some of the techniques described above, you may engage their minds in more challenging work later in the lesson. Try to encourage pupils of all abilities to access some primary or complex sources. Harris (2005) has argued that when reading a difficult text, it has been found that it is better to try to bring the text alive for pupils rather than simplify it. If your lesson involves lots of active learning and pupil talk, you are less likely to need different resources. Decision-making games are an example of an activity that may appeal to everyone. It is usually the written tasks that need to be differentiated.

Consider what you are aiming to achieve in your lesson and through a particular task. Is it possible for all pupils to access the same knowledge, and employ the same skills at their own level, or do they need different tasks and materials in order to produce their best work? Assuming the need for some matching of tasks to ability, four possible methods are considered in Table 8.2. Support for the less able and extension and enrichment for the more able are dealt with separately.

Table 8.2 Methods of differentiation

Method of differentiation	How it can be used	Comments
1 Questions printed in ascending order of difficulty.	For any worksheet – you simply need to rearrange the tasks on it. Questions could be directly targeted to specific National Curriculum levels, so that pupils can begin at a chosen point (see website for guidance).	All pupils given the same materials – may help avoid stigma of giving out easy work to less able pupils. However, they may become disheartened that they never finish the sheet, and may be tempted to attempt tasks that are too difficult. More able pupils do not have to waste time completing the simplest tasks.
2 Different resources.	Textbooks and other resources designed for different abilities. Some textbooks now come with packs of supplementary worksheets, which are differentiated.	The work is done for you. Can you use different textbooks simultaneously in the classroom? Use of Foundation/Higher textbooks may follow well from a starter involving everyone.
3 Ability groups.	Pupils could work on the same task, so that differentiation is achieved by outcome. Or they could study different aspects of a topic, or different tasks could be given to each group.	This may prevent more able pupils from lowering their expectations. You need to know the group quite well. Takes a lot of preparation. May require changes in seating plan. May lead to behavioural problems.
4 Different tasks for different pupils. These can be given out by the teacher or selected by pupils (see lesson plan on website).	Worksheets can be produced on two or three levels. They could be labelled Higher/Foundation or A/B, etc.	Most pupils are able to choose wisely for themselves which task to attempt. Gives them some control over their own learning. Involves a lot of work, but is more easily managed as part of a team. Can be particularly useful for homework booklets or sheets or important assessments. However, less able pupils may feel a stigma in taking a lower level worksheet – can you make them look similar if this is the case? Takes time to distribute sheets, and cannot be done by a pupil.

Support materials for least able

Here are some guiding principles.

1   Avoid copying charts, timelines or long sections of writing from the board. Transferring information can be difficult. Instead provide pupils with a printed chart or timeline to fill in. Copying, if necessary, is more easily done from a sheet with large print on the desk.

2   Model how to set out answers. Less able pupils often lack confidence in how to approach a task, and especially in how to begin.

3   Reduce the amount of writing by providing charts to fill in for comparisons or source analysis, or graphs. For example, use a graph to show changing attitudes in the First World War where date is plotted against morale (from positive to negative) (see website). Pupils add labels to show why attitudes changed, instead of writing in paragraphs. Or use a chart like the one on the website, for source analysis.

4   Sources can be annotated, instead of written about.

5   Give pupils highlighter pens to pick out key parts of texts, instead of writing about them.

6   Remove or explain complicated words and language structures.

7   Use large font and pictures to break up text.

8   Support writing using writing frames, starters, connectives, topic sentences and key words. Introduce target language structures with rewards for using them. Extended writing can be built up by sorting cards under various headings. Give pupils topic sentences for a paragraph about each of the headings or allow them to compose these sentences in groups. They then use the other cards to write the rest of the paragraph.

9   Give out help sheets to supplement work done by the rest of the class (see website). This may include memory prompts, multi-choice answers, a cloze passage, tick boxes. Pupils with very low levels of English or severe special needs may be given some of the answers to copy. The advantage of this approach is that supplementary materials can be given out with the minimum of fuss and are useful for homework. Pupils can be given the choice of a 'help sheet' if they are struggling with a task. Thus they feel that they can complete the same work as the rest of the class, and can access homework, but also see progress at the point where they no longer need the help sheet.

Extension and enrichment for the more able

Below is some guidance on how to meet the needs of your more able pupils. They may be especially useful in a mixed ability classroom:

1   Extra reading and research at home or in class. Try to build up your own bank of resources during your PGCE year and as your career progresses.

2   Allow more independence in approaching a task, e.g. finding own books, page numbers or websites for research, planning how to proceed with a project.

3   Higher-order questions, e.g. Ask, 'How did the people of Leningrad survive the siege?' instead of 'What was it like to live through the siege?'

4   Devising mind maps and concept maps (Fisher, 2002). These maps can be produced by less able pupils, maybe with the help of a map which you have started. More able pupils will be able to show more independence in choosing key ideas, and showing links between them.

5   Look at the broader picture by reference to other events in history or in current affairs. (KSU 2d) Regarding the atomic bomb, you could ask if they can think of other difficult decisions which leaders have been required to justify afterwards. Encourage them to devise arguments, engage in debate, and analyse why you have made certain comparisons.

6   Select groups of pupils to summarise learning and present it to the class, or ask them to prepare tasks for the rest of the class.

7   Work based on high level thinking and reasoning, e.g. mysteries (Activity 8.3 following Fisher (2002)). These involve giving pupils a number of clues, usually printed on separate cards. The pupils have to use the clues to solve a mystery. These are best based on true stories from the past, perhaps referring to an individual rather than an event. Some of the clues may be red herrings, while some will be more useful than others, so that a lot of classification and discussion is required. Mysteries are also accessible for less able pupils, who can be given fewer cards and more teacher guidance, or a sheet to prompt them. See Becket example on website.

Activity 8.3   Resources

1   Think of a story that could be made into a mystery. Devise fifteen statements about it to form the cards given to pupils. Then select eight cards for a pack for less able pupils. Shorten them or simplify the vocabulary.

2   Take a worksheet used in your department and devise a help sheet to supplement it. This could include explanation of key words, multi-choice answers or gap fills where the correct answer is selected or completed on the help sheet and then copied on to the main worksheet (or into an exercise book). The example of a differentiated homework on the website includes a help sheet.

Now try Activity 8.4 which is designed to help you to identify the principles and characteristics which underpin the activities listed above to enable you to apply to a variety of content, skills and concepts.

Activity 8.4   Teaching the able pupil

1   Study the activities for the able pupil described in on p. 76. Make a list of the characteristics of the able pupil, which are implicit in these activities.

_____

_____

_____

_____

2   Compare your list with those set out in Figure 7.1 on p. 168 of *Learning to Teach History in the Secondary School*. To what extent do the activities listed faithfully reflect the theory?

_____

_____

_____

_____

Activity 8.4 *continued*

3   Using your placement school history department syllabus for one of the KS3 years, try to identify content, which would be appropriate for the activities listed below.

(i) for devising higher order questions	
(ii) for devising mind maps and concept maps	
(iii) for making links with other periods and current events	
(iv) good topics for debate, mounting arguments	
(v) for class presentations	

4   Think of an extension project, which you could set for gifted and able pupils, based on extra reading and independent additional research, including the use of websites, and involving some planning of the task by the pupil.

ENGLISH AS AN ADDITIONAL LANGUAGE (EAL)

For pupils with EAL, try to find out about their national and linguistic background, previous schooling and level of ability (Activity 8.5). You may encounter pupils with high levels of numeracy or memory, for example, who could be doing well in subjects such as mathematics. You may teach pupils whose first language has a different alphabet, or even those who have never learned to read and write. Those with a very basic command of English cannot access the history curriculum in the usual way. They may be withdrawn from your lessons, but often are not. Some strategies to help are as follows:

- Aim to include pupils in the lesson, even by inviting them to give out books. It is often better to speak and especially to give encouragement, so that the pupil does not feel too isolated even if he/she understands very little. This may also help ensure that they have more confidence to speak to you when they do begin to acquire more English.
- Pair pupils with a peer interpreter who can explain points and tasks in their own language. Be clear with the interpreter about how you wish this to work.
- Ask someone (EMAS department, older pupil) to translate key terms or instructions

---

Activity 8.5 EAL resources

1 Find out from class teachers what they know about pupils with EAL in the classes you are taking. Does the school provide written analysis of this?

2 Find out from the history department if there are any cultural or religious sensitivities of which you should be aware. For example, you may cause offence by asking a strict Muslim to draw a picture of a person.

3 Find out about the EMAS department in the school where you work. What kind of support are they providing for pupils, and can you refer pupils for help with homework, and so on? Can they advise you on specific linguistic difficulties experienced by speakers of particular languages?

4 With the permission of a teacher in the school where you are working, analyse pupils' written work. Make a note of examples of use of second language influence, for example in the use of pluperfect tense instead of simple past (e.g. 'Thomas Becket had gone to France', instead of 'Thomas Becket went to France'). Consider ways of addressing these language issues.

5 Try to arrange to speak with a pupil or group of pupils who have EAL, but have enough English to chat with you informally. Ask what difficulties they have encountered in learning, especially in history.

6 Consider any analogies that you have heard teachers make in observation or have made yourself in teaching. Common examples are references to football, well-known buildings and places, or current affairs. Consider which groups of pupils may find these meaningless or even confusing. Is it still worth using them if you can reach some pupils in the class, if not all? Can you think of analogies that may be appropriate for all pupils in your school?

---

into the foreign language. Write them on to your resources, so that they can be re-used.

• Use simplified language and visual resources, while working on building up literacy skills.

• Use labelling and colouring drawings, pictures to reinforce vocabulary, matching words and meanings, completing sentences based on a short text or even copying in order to engage pupils in some way in your topic.

• For pupils who speak English well, but are not so good at writing it, invite them to give oral presentations to the class. They may have been accustomed to this in a different country.

• Where possible, consider the implications of inclusion in the curriculum. Is there any possibility to teach topics that relate to the background of your pupils, or for them to research it as homework? If this is not possible, it is important to let them know that our society has always been diverse. In our department, we have introduced a project on settlers and invaders. We start in Year 7 with a look at the first millennium when pupils see that our roots come from a variety of different places, and begin to think about what it is to be British. We follow this up chronologically in Year 8 and 9 until we get to post-World War II immigration. For a homework pupils have to find out a family story, and relate it to the class. We get some very interesting stories from all over the world, and pupils often delve into their family history for the first time. The principles of good history teaching, which educate pupils to look at events from more than one point of view, should help in the process of inclusion. When teaching topics that could be culturally sensitive, such as the slave trade or the Crusades, try to find sources from different points of view. It is important when teaching the slave trade or the Holocaust to present the slaves or the Jews not simply as victims, but as survivors and resistance fighters at times. In the interests of inclusion, it is also worth noting that the white British people were not all bad at this time, and that black Africans also played a role in capturing slaves for example. White people, such as French prisoners of war, were sometimes also transported across the Atlantic as slaves.

SUMMARY

Inclusion is one of the most challenging tasks facing history teachers, but it is well worth spending time on in order to help pupils achieve their best and to ensure smooth classroom management. There is no simple solution to meeting the needs of all pupils. Most pupils, however, recognise when your approach and planning have attempted to include them, and will respond well to your teaching. In the early stages of the course, you should begin to understand the needs of pupils and start to address them. Later you should try to develop confidence in meeting the needs of a wide range of pupils by adapting resources and preparing you own. As you evaluate your lessons, you will became aware of which approaches work and which do not. You will learn how to adapt schemes of work and lesson plans, and over time you will build up your own bank of resources.

FURTHER READING

Brien, T. (2001), *Enabling Inclusion: Blue Skies . . . Dark Clouds*, Norwich: The Stationery Office.

Cunnah, W. (2000) 'History teaching, literacy and special educational needs', Chapter 9 in J. Arthur and R. Phillips (eds) *Issues in History Teaching*, London: Routledge.

Fisher, P. (ed.) (2002) *Thinking Through History*, Cambridge: Chris Kingston Publishing, Chapters 3, 5 and 7.

Hammond, K. (1999) 'And Joe arrives . . . stretching the very able pupil in the mixed ability classroom', *Teaching History*, 94.

Harris, R. (2005) 'Does differentiation have to mean different?', *Teaching History*, 118.

Harris, R. and Luff, I. (2004) *Meeting Special Needs in the Curriculum: History*, London: David Fulton Publishers.

Chapter 9 ICT

Using presentation technology

BILL SMITH

INTRODUCTION

The demand that ICT should be incorporated into all areas of the curriculum seems to be irresistible and indeed, as time passes, gathers pace still further. This insistence applies to the teaching of history equally as to other disciplines. The use of ICT needs to be seen as an integral part of the whole package of skills and strategies which can be deployed to enhance teaching and learning *in history*, rather than, as is perhaps more often the case, a discreet area of experience or expertise which can be 'ticked off' as part of the satisfaction of external standards.

This requires consideration of ICT at two levels. First, it is necessary to audit and subsequently to enhance, as necessary, the skill levels of all trainee teachers. The types of basic ICT skills, which enable the user to construct and deploy resources and exercises in widely used applications such as PowerPoint, Excel or Word, can very easily be acquired. The second component of training for the use of ICT in history must be the consideration of when, how and why to incorporate new technologies into the delivery of history. It cannot be assumed that the need for this aspect of training will reduce in proportion to the rising level of technical competence. In using new technology to enhance the teaching of history, as in so many other things, knowing *what* to do may be less important than having a clear understanding of *when*, *how* and *why* it should be done. It is this latter dimension, rather than the skills aspect, which is the aim of this chapter, which will focus primarily on whole-class teaching using a data projector, rather than on the use of ICT by individual pupils. (For a useful description of activities involving pupil presentations, see *History, ICT and Learning in the Secondary School*, Chapter 7, Routledge, 2001).

Chapter aims

By the end of the chapter you should be able to:

- understand the limitations and the advantages of using presentation technology;
- audit your own current skills in the use of presentation technology in your teaching;
- create a range of practical approaches that can be used with whole classes at different times during the lesson, such as ICT-based starters;
- adapt for your own content the key characteristics of effective activities using presentation technology;
- understand the uses that can be made of hyperlinks;
- identify ways in which presentation technology can be used to enhance your teaching of historical skills such as source analysis and historical interpretations.

THE LIMITATIONS AND ADVANTAGES OF USING ICT IN HISTORY

Limitations

First of all, let us face some facts, however unpalatable they may be:

- ☹ Having £3,000-worth of ICT equipment dangling from your ceiling and hanging on your wall will NOT solve all your problems.
- ☹ There is NOT a button which you can press which will deliver a perfect lesson.
- ☹ You WILL still have to work hard and be creative to come up with engaging and interesting ideas for your lessons.
- ☹ You WILL find that, at first, your new 'friend' will actually *create* work rather than reduce it.
- ☹ It WILL take time to find out *what* it can do (take my advice and don't – for Heaven's sake – try to work out *how* it does it).
- ☹ You WILL simply have to put some time into practising and tinkering with your new toys – that's the only way to find out what really works for you.
- ☹ You WILL find that, on occasion, you will be seduced by the power of the medium and neglect the *history* content of your lesson in favour of the latest technological trick, which you have just mastered.
- ☹ You WILL fall into the trap of 'death by PowerPoint'. As long as you recognise it before you have gone too far down the road of endless slides of text, you will be able to salvage some excellent lesson resources.

Advantages

Think about what you would like your projector to allow you to do.

- ☺ Would you like to have high quality, full colour images to show to students? (Or do you prefer to have them squinting at a dodgy old black and white photocopy?).
- ☺ Would you like to be able to put simple instructions and lesson aims in colour and displayed at the press of a key? (Or do you prefer writing out those instructions time and again?).
- ☺ Would you like to have starters and plenaries displayed simply by pressing a key? (Or do you want to have to spend valuable time writing them out on the white board time and again?).
- ☺ Do you want to be able to display some of the brilliant material available on the Internet (while avoiding the rubbish) . . . and get the students to interact with it? (even if you don't have an interactive white board there are plenty of opportunities).
- ☺ Would you like to play a video or DVD and have it so that everyone in the class can actually see it?

These are just a few of the simple things that might get you started.

The remainder of this chapter makes some practical suggestions on how new opportunities provided by the application of technology might be used to enhance the teaching and learning of history.

Although it may now have been overtaken by more sophisticated formulae, it seems appropriate to deploy the good old three-part lesson structure (starter activity, main lesson tasks, plenary) for the remainder of this discussion. First, then, we might usefully consider the ways in which both starter and plenary activities can be enhanced by the use of a projector. Second, we can take a look at some possible uses of presentation technologies to enhance and support a range of activities.

STARTER AND PLENARY ACTIVITIES

Looking first at starter and plenary activities, the key point to be reiterated is that none of the starter and plenary suggestions, which are offered here require the use of an interactive white board. In some cases access to an interactive board would enhance the ways in which they might be used and would allow both teacher and pupil greater flexibility in the ways in which they interact with the material. However, they are all constructed so that they can be used to good effect with a projector and a standard white board.

There are several preliminary points, which need to be made about the suggestions. First, they are all 'real' examples and in this way represent a response to the call for the need of 'eminently practicable, tried and tested materials' by Terry Haydn in Chapter 8 of *Issues in Teaching History* (Routledge, 2000). They have all been used by me and colleagues, in real classrooms, with real pupils, and they have been found to work. Some work very well, some less so, but all are worth considering. Second, they are easy to construct in the first instance and, even more importantly, easy to adapt and amend to different topics, different age or ability groups and different school contexts. While, in the main, they are described here as 'starters', they can also be very effectively deployed as plenary activities. Third, they were designed with very clear objectives in mind.

The key function of the starters is to engage pupils in the crucial opening phases of the lesson. It may seem banal, but it needs to be remembered that the key function of starter activities is to assist pupils in their efforts to learn. In this I am applying Haydn's principles for the use of ICT that:

1   Pupils must be asked to do something with the resources they are presented with rather than simply being provided with access to an increased volume of historical information.
2   There should be some valid historical purpose to the activities that pupils are engaged in.

I believe it is appropriate to suggest key characteristics of effective starter activities under the acronym '*LEARN*'.

First, the activities should be '*Low maintenance*' from the teacher's point of view. Starters need to be constructed so as to allow pupils initially to understand and proceed with their task with minimal reference to, or intervention from, the teacher. This is where the use of the projector is an enormous advantage. Even relatively simple starter tasks take up valuable time to write on the board, whereas a pre-prepared task can be activated in a matter of seconds. Simple tasks such as compiling an acrostic based on a keyword, or solving an anagram to identify a keyword can be delivered in glorious technicolor, with accompanying graphics.

Second, starter activities need to be '*engaging*'. The engagement can also be facilitated by the quality and clarity of the material itself. Again, this is where the projector scores heavily over other means of delivery. The immediate availability of clear, colourful text, with high quality images, and perhaps also sound and moving images, attracts and retains pupils' attention far more readily. A difficult concept can thus be made to appear relevant, with the added bonus that, the PowerPoint presentation being automated, it can be carried forward with minimal teacher intervention.

The third point to be borne in mind is that starters should be '*accessible*' to all members of the class. This does not mean reducing issues to a lowest common denominator. Rather, it means providing a stimulus or a set task, which can be approached at different levels of complexity and by different routes.

It is fundamental that the starter activity should be '*relevant*' to the content of the lesson. The starter tasks need to be a fundamental part of the overall lesson objectives, rather than simply something bolted on at the beginning to get pupils' attention. This does not mean that the lesson objective should be viewed as a straitjacket into which the starter must be squeezed. The relevance to the main activity of the lesson can sometimes be fairly tangential; it is up to the teacher to decide upon the nature of the links, which they wish to create. Seemingly generic tasks such as creating words from a selection of letters can be given curriculum relevance simply by highlighting a keyword, which will then become a focus point for the lesson. Starter tasks can just as easily refer back to previous learning as they can refer forward to, as yet, undeveloped areas. The nine-letter 'trackword' format, which features in the *Radio Times* for example can easily be replicated with great clarity and be used not only to identify a keyword, but also to encourage a flexibility in handling words. The possibilities for simple, yet very effective, topic-specific starters are almost limitless.

Starters are often most effective in contributing to overall lesson objectives when they are constructed so as to require *'no special materials'*. If the starter needs to be accompanied by even something so simple as a worksheet or a textbook, let alone anything more complex, then some of those key functions, which have been discussed above can be compromised. The projected image or text negates the need for a textbook or worksheet (it can also save a fortune on photocopying). Time spent in distributing materials detracts from the engagement of members of the class on their task or from the teacher's ability to manage pro-actively particular individuals or the class as a whole. Most of the starters suggested in Table 9.1 require nothing more, in terms of materials, than an exercise book and a pen. What they are intended to require, and to stimulate, are the engagement, interest and attention of pupils.

Table 9.1 Examples of starters using ICT

Purpose	Description	Task
1 To encourage students to speculate on the use of propaganda in Elizabethan England	Display a rolling PowerPoint of a modern iconic figure (David Beckham perhaps?), which portray different 'roles'. Follow with a second sequence of Elizabethan portraits (e.g. Armada, Rainbow, Ditchley portraits).	Students could be asked to supply a caption appropriate to each image, thus 'summarising' the message intended to be conveyed or think of 3–5 adjectives, which each image brings to mind.
2 To introduce a keyword, which will be the focus of the lesson content. This task also helps to foster an increased mental dexterity in handling language.	Present, in full colour and attractive font, a grid of letters containing the scrambled word.	Students are asked to identify the keyword.
3 To make links between key aspects of lesson content. For example, on the Treaty of Versailles.	Display a series of words, portraits or images of objects, for a limited time and in random order. The images might be Lloyd George, Wilson, Clemenceau and Kaiser Wilhelm, for example.	Students are asked to identify either the 'odd one out' in any sequence, or to reorder the elements into a more useful sequence.

Activity 9.2 comprises a set of activities based on slides on a PowerPoint file encouraging a range of tried and tested approaches to starting lessons.

WHOLE CLASS ACTIVITIES

In terms of whole-class teaching, PowerPoint, I would argue, is most effective when it is used in very simple ways to engage attention and to stimulate thought, speculation and discussion, rather than as a vehicle to convey large amounts of information. This is where presentation software, such as PowerPoint, can sometimes be used inappropriately. We have all, I am

Activity 9.1   ICT starters

1   Imagine that you have a group to teach who habitually arrive late, and in dribs and drabs, to your lesson. Make a list of ways in which the use of ICT could improve the start of your lesson.

2   Think of a starter task, which you have used, which requires teacher explanation and printed materials for it to be completed; work out ways in which it can be done with neither of these, through the medium of ICT.

3   Identify key images for each of the main topic areas, which you have taught. Think of ways in which you could use them, displayed in full colour via a projector, as lesson starters.

Activity 9.2   Developing starter activities using ICT

1   Access: http://www.routledge.com/textbooks/9780415370240 and the mmustarters.ppt file.
There you will find 16 slides of exemplar material for the classroom.

2   Select slide 1. Write down and complete using the details of one of your recent lessons.

3   Select slide 3. Using an acrostic. Select a keyword from each of your last three lessons and attempt the task yourself. What type of keyword works best with this starter?

4   Select slide 4. Using the same keywords as above, attempt this task yourself. How many questions can you formulate?

5   What are the advantages and limitations of each of the approaches illustrated on these slides?

6   In what ways do you think these ideas could be developed and changed for different ability groups?

sure, sat through seemingly interminable PowerPoint presentations where a series of slides, packed with text, follow each other with a dreadful and mind-numbing inevitability. There can be a particular danger in presentations of this nature as they can impose a sort of 'electronic straitjacket' where slide 2 must follow slide 1, before we then move on to slides 3 to 27, with no scope for adaptation or diversion depending on the response of the pupils. For pupils, there is a danger that 'death by worksheet' might simply be exchanged for a version of 'death by electronic worksheet', in the form of information presentations, some of which, if you're lucky, might have an accompanying graphic or task.

More importantly, this linear use of PowerPoint slides does not fit neatly into the way pupils learn. Good classroom discussion rarely follows in a neat logical pattern, but can move from point to point in a random and tangential manner. However, by using the 'hyperlink' facility within the software, it is possible to jump from slide to slide in a way, which mirrors more closely classroom interactions. Hyperlinks create links to other slides within the presentation, which do not need to be accessed sequentially. In addition, hyperlinks can be made to the Internet websites and other media.

Thus PowerPoint really scores when it provides a degree of flexibility in the delivery of information, which is not available by other media. To take a simple example, consider a Year 7 class learning about the weapons and equipment used by the Roman army. It is relatively simple task to construct a PowerPoint presentation based upon a single image of a Roman soldier which will allow a class to speculate about the function of different parts of the soldier's kit and, to investigate them in a sequence of their choosing. All that is required is to create hyperlinks from different parts of the main image to a series of information slides, which would provide a detailed commentary on each element. These slides would most obviously contain static images and text, but might also incorporate short video clips. Other applications might be in analysing the layout of a First World War trench or an 'interactive' map of England during the Civil Wars.

Presentation technology can be used very effectively to examine or deconstruct both images and text in a way that would be more difficult, and less engaging, though by no means impossible, by more traditional means. Take, for example, a still image of an event like Peterloo. It is perfectly possible to have pupils examine a black-and-white photocopied image of the scene. The ability to support them with a high-quality full-colour image displayed via the projector makes the task immediately both more engaging and more fulfilling. Furthermore, it then allows pupils to work co-operatively to comment upon, discuss and annotate the image. Without access to an interactive white board the annotation can, of course, simply be achieved by writing or drawing 'on top of' the projected image. If used in conjunction with an interactive whiteboard the annotations can themselves be saved for future reference. Furthermore, it is also rewarding to explore the potential of using the 'autoshapes' menu to insert 'speech' or 'thought' bubble captions to images (events such as Munich, the Nazi–Soviet Pact, a picture of the 'Big Three' at Yalta, Potsdam). Activity 9.3 shows how a hyperlink presentation can be created with follow-up activities.

Activity 9.3 Using hyperlinks

Access http://www.routledge.com/textbooks/9780415370240

There you will find a stage by stage exercise, using an image of Peterloo, which will help you to develop your skill in using a visual source. When you have completed the tasks, you may wish to consider the following key questions:

1　What benefits can be gained from this approach?
2　What might be the potential problems in the classroom for you as a teacher and how might they be overcome?
3　Bearing in mind the danger of pupil passivity as well as information overload, consider the role of the pupils. How can they be actively involved; how might they formulate questions about the material? How might they record some of the information?
4　Once you have developed the skill of using hyperlinks, there are a range of possibilities available to you for using the facility for class interaction involving decision-making. Consider some of those decision-making exercises used with duplicated sheets or card sorts and then how hyperlinks might be used as an alternative:

　(i)　How could hyperlinks be used for decision-making for the understanding of cause and consequence and of interpretations?
　(ii)　How could you use the facility for the pupils to consider 'what if' questions?

Some examples of such uses of hyperlinks may be seen on the chapter's website.

The subject of such analysis need not simply be a still image, whether acquired from the Internet or scanned from a printed source. It is equally possible to examine single images or a sequence of images extracted from a video or DVD clip. At the simplest level, simply pause the clip at the required point. To allow for a little more control, it may be better to extract the precise image from a DVD and convert it into a static format.

Such collaborative, close analysis techniques can equally well be applied to text sources as to images. The attention of the whole class can of course by other means easily be focused upon a single word or phrase. However, if the text extract is displayed as a 'Word' file, for example, pupils can be invited to experiment with changing words, reorganising construction, adding or deleting text, introducing new adjectives to change meaning, highlighting keywords, seeking out bias in the use of language: all of them in such a way as can be easily saved or deleted as required. Pupils can be given access to either mediated interaction with the text by instructing either the teacher or a nominated individual to make the changes suggested, or to direct interaction, perhaps by their use of a wireless keyboard and mouse.

Crucially, such analysis can be 'provisional', allowing thoughts to be re-examined, revised and expanded, without the fear of having committed to an answer, which turns out to be 'wrong'. Given that the majority of pupils, of all abilities, are greatly exercised by the need to have the 'right' answers, this capacity to allow them to speculate and to share ideas before committing themselves to a definitive answer can be a powerful learning tool.

Activity 9.4 demonstrates how to use the projector for source analysis and evaluation. This diversion into the means of 'interaction' raises a key point, which needs to be addressed when constructing and deploying whole-class teaching activities using ICT. The widely used label 'interactive white board' can, I feel, be somewhat misleading. In facilitating the learning of a whole class a skilled teacher will strive to 'interact' with all students during the ebb and flow of a particular phase of a lesson, and may well also be interested in developing interactions among and between individuals or groups of students (Activity 9.5). There can be a danger that the 'interactive white board', if not used carefully, actually becomes a medium of interaction only between the technology itself and one chosen individual, or, even more dangerously, between the technology and the teacher, with the students as spectators, rather than as active participants. Some applications and tasks which have a superficial attraction,

---

Activity 9.4   Using the projector to stimulate source analysis and evaluation

Access http://www.routledge.com/textbooks/9780415370240
   Open the Word file about Queen Mary.

1   Devise a series of routines, which could be used in whole class teaching involving:

   (i)   highlighting a single word or phrase;
   (ii)   adding/deleting words to change meaning;
   (iii)   identifying bias;
   (iv)   what words or phrases are the most important for the historian?

2   (i)   Select slide 15 from the mmustarters.ppt file on the website, which shows a diagram called 'Judgement Cake':
   (ii)   Consider how this slide could be used for the discussion of the relative importance of phrase in the above source.
   (iii)   Consider how this slide could be used for other key elements such as cause, consequence and significance.

Activity 9.5 Using ICT for interpretation

1   Take one double page from a textbook of your choice. Plan a sequence of three PowerPoint slides, which could deliver the same information in a more engaging manner.

2   Choose a short piece of newsreel footage from the First or Second World War, which has a strong propaganda element in its commentary. Write your own commentary for the same clip, which gives an opposite interpretation of the images shown. How could you use ICT to allow you to illustrate the fact that the same images are capable of differing interpretations?

3   Find or create 'model' answers for a typical GCSE question, which illustrate different levels of response. How could whole-class presentation technology be used to help students identify the best answers?

4   Make a conscious attempt to build up 'collections' of images on particular themes, concepts, events or people. (For example, a collection of images of Elizabeth II from her accession to the throne to the present day can be a powerful way of showing that the image of the monarchy changes over time.)

5   As a group, 'sub-contract' the mining of particular history websites to build up a collection of 'best bits' or 'gems' which you can then share with colleagues.

---

arising out of their attractive graphics or clever construction, can prove to be counter-productive in whole-class teaching as they restrict the role played by all but those who are directly involved with the technology.

Activity 9.6 includes further activities using the PowerPoint file associated with this chapter.

Activity 9.6 Using PowerPoint in plenaries and lesson endings

1   Access the starters.ppt file.

2   Select slide 14, which shows a method of using self-assessment in the class-room. Consider a lesson you have recently observed or taught. How could that lesson be applied to the information on this slide?

3   In what ways could you adapt and develop this idea in the context of Assessment for Learning?

4   Select slide 2. Using a current lesson plan, what would the completed slide look like? What are the advantages and disadvantages of this use of PowerPoint?

SUMMARY

While not in any way attempting to offer a definitive or all-embracing answer to the issues arising from the deployment of new technologies, it would be useful to offer a few concluding thoughts. First and foremost, it is essential to view ICT as a means to an end, rather than as an end in itself, when it comes to teaching and learning in history. It must be remembered and periodically reinforced, even to oneself, that the PowerPoint show, or the word processing task or the drag and drop exercise must be the means to deliver appropriate content rather than becoming, itself, the focus of the learning experience.

There are certainly some instances when the allure of the technology itself can be used to engage and motivate students. The anticipation and excitement, which one can generate by dangling the carrot of 'a lesson in the computer room' are likely to remain until such time as access to computers within subject areas is greatly enhanced. As a general rule, however, the technology should be 'transparent'. That is to say, the means of delivery should not obscure the historical learning, which is intended. Ideally, maintaining the optical metaphor, the technology should in point of fact be used in such a way as to bring the historical content or concept into a sharper focus than could be achieved by other means. We do a disservice both to pupils and to the technology itself if we simply use ICT because 'we're supposed to', in order to place a tick in the appropriate box. If something works really well without any technology required, then why use any? If you cannot identify a way, through the shared expertise and experience of yourself and others, in which technology would enhance the learning, which you want students to experience then don't feel constrained to use it. On the other hand, do stay receptive to the possibilities which already exist and which are expanding all the time. There are excellent examples of the use of ICT in history available in many areas; seek them out, borrow them and refine their use so that they become powerful 'high-impact' resources, which work well.

ACKNOWLEDGEMENT

Activity 9.3 and the associated website materials were devised by Christopher Chambers. Thanks to Terry Haydn for suggesting the last two tasks in Activity 9.5.

FURTHER READING

Haydn, T. (2000), 'Information and communications technology in the history classroom', in J. Arthur and R. Phillips (eds) *Issues in History Teaching*, London: Routledge.

Haydn, T. and Counsell, C. (eds) (2003) *History, ICT and Learning in the Secondary School*, London: Routledge.

Walsh, B. (2005) *Exciting ICT in History*, Network Educational Press.

Chapter 10 Peer assessment

IAN DICKSEE AND MARTIN HUNT

INTRODUCTION

Assessment has become one of the most difficult, arguably the most difficult, aspect of the work of the history teacher. Not least because the whole topic of assessment in history has given rise to a whole series of debates, some quite heated, and all interconnected. To the established history teacher, assessment might seem a series of compromises, while the trainee history teacher could well be mystified by the apparent mismatch between common practice in schools and the published documentation about assessing progress in history.

This chapter will seek to give you an overview of some of the current debates about the assessment of learning in history and to provide guidance, using the example of lessons on King John to a mixed ability Year 7 class, on the use of peer assessment within the context of those debates.

Chapter aims

By the end of this chapter you should be able to:

- have an understanding of the current debates and challenges involved in the assessment of pupils' progress in history including the use of levels;
- understand the arguments favouring the use of peer assessment in history;
- devise criteria and documentation for the use of peer assessment;
- understand the procedures involved in implementing peer assessment.

ASSESSMENT IN HISTORY

The current debates on assessment in history cover many areas, some of which may be briefly summarised. They include concerns about the external examinations. A recent Historical Association Report (2005, p. 30) notes that three such concerns here are the decline of teacher assessment associated with the reduction of coursework, the quality of the questions on the examination papers and the limited range of the types of assessment. A particular worry is that the assessment tasks bear little relationship to actual historical practice. Over the years mark schemes have become predictable and have encouraged mechanistic responses. How sources are used for assessment is a particular concern where candidates are expected to reach considerable judgements on very small extracts.

Mark schemes, whether used for external examinations or for use in school, feature highly in many debates. Most indicate levels of attainment but they can invite a host of questions. One of the most intense debates surrounds the use of the National Curriculum levels for mark schemes even for small pieces of work used for formative assessment. While many teachers and advisers feel that such levels are inappropriate for such assessment and that it was never intended they should be used in this way, there are often pressures within a school from senior managers for the use of these levels as an indication of progress (see *Teaching History*, June 2004, for some thought-provoking articles). Teachers feel obliged to supply them. Their frustration is increased by the awareness that the progression implicit in the National Curriculum levels as well as the published examination mark schemes, assume models of progression that are highly contentious. Lee and Shemilt (2003) have shown that the development of understanding in history is much more complex than this and that progress between and within the Key Elements often occurs at different rates. There exists also a general unease that the process of studying history cannot be so easily compartmentalised and that often an indicator of progress is the ability to accommodate several of the Key Elements within one piece of work.

Nevertheless if assessment is to be used to discriminate, then there has to be some form of standardisation. It is often far easier to fault current practice than it is to replace it. Hence the attempt to provide mark schemes which are easily understood by both teachers and examiners (Activity 10.1).

Activity 10.1   Assessment within the school

Where do these debates about assessment leave you, the trainee teacher? Clearly you need to know about them as they will soon, if not already, influence the way you think and plan your teaching. It is useful to begin with your placement schools' assessment policies and practices:

1   Through your mentor, arrange a meeting with the teacher in charge of school assessment for a discussion about school policies and the requirements made of each department.
2   Discuss with your mentor or Head of Department the history department's approach to assessment both yearly and at the Key Stages. Ask to see examples of tests set in the past, how achievement is recorded and how it is communicated to the parents.
3   Consider how these discussions relate to the debates listed briefly above.

Activity 10.2 will enable you to become familiar with levels of marking schemes, the National Curriculum levels and to attempt an analysis of both in relation to the progression implied.

In spite of the many concerns about current practice, there are many positive developments in assessment taking place in schools. Included in these is a movement towards the greater use of self-assessment and peer assessment. With the recent launch of *Assessment for Learning* as the leading priority in the *National KS3 Strategy in Secondary Schools*, peer assessment is already becoming an established practice in many classrooms. The value of this assessment technique to both teachers and pupils must not be underestimated and rightly deserves its place within the *Assessment for Learning* framework. Giving pupils the opportunity to understand exactly where they are in their learning and what they need to do next to progress, encourages them to become reflective and independent learners that are confident with the assessment process.

Activity 10.2 Analysing levels in history

1   Ask your mentor or your Head of Department if you may see the published mark schemes for the GCSE examination used by the department. Choose three schemes, which target three different assessment objectives – causation, interpretations and the use of sources and then analyse the progression they use. Does any pattern emerge? Are there significant leaps between levels? What flexibility is there for alternative, parallel or unexpected responses?

2   Using the National Curriculum levels statement for history, do a similar analysis of the relevant sentences for those same concepts. Again, what is the basis for the progression?

3   Consider the similarities and the differences in the use of levels by the two documents.

4   Read Lee and Shemilt (2003), 'A scaffold not a cage; progression and progression models in history', *Teaching History*, 113.

Effective peer assessment relies, fundamentally, on the pupils' understanding of the success criteria of the work being assessed. Providing this guidance in a format the pupils can understand is essential if peer assessment is to be successful. Only then can pupils provide their peers with supported judgements as to where they are in their learning, and then be able to identify their next steps (Activity 10.3). The value of this process is enhanced by students responding to their peers' evaluation of their performance with further self-assessment of the progress they have made.

EXEMPLAR LESSONS

The lessons described below intend to show that peer assessment could be particularly effective for the teaching and learning of history. It can provide a valuable method of assessing real understanding in contrast to rote and superficial learning as well as formulaic responses. For a subject, which seeks to integrate knowledge with specific skills and concepts, it helps to provide excellent opportunities for pupils to discuss and display their understanding.

However, with reference to the debates described above, history has its problems. Again, many of these derive from uncertainties about progression and the problem of levels, National Curriculum or otherwise. While Byrom's (2003) 'climbing frame' is probably a more accurate analogy for progression than a 'success ladder', it is also very sophisticated. For peer assessment to succeed pupils need clear straightforward descriptions of what it is they

---

Activity 10.3 The use of peer assessment

1   Discuss with members of the history department to which you are attached when and how the department makes use of peer assessment.
2   Discuss the value of its use in approaches other than written work such as pupil presentations, role play, displays and in situations where pupils are given the opportunity to help to devise assessment criteria.
3   How is the ability to assess their peers developed over time? For example, by giving pupils two pieces of work and asking them in pairs to decide which was the better and to explain why.
4   What do the department feel are the strengths and limitations of using this form of assessment with the learning of second-order concepts such as cause, change, evidence and interpretations?

---

have to achieve. So what follows is what many teachers find they have to do – a compromise but with the prospect of moving on to using statements of achievement that are more satisfying, being both topic and concept specific. Furthermore, the chapter, designed for trainees, is as much, if not more, concerned with the process of using peer assessment as it is with legitimate concerns about levels.

Context of the assessment

One of five key assessments used with Year 7 at our school focuses on the key question, 'Was King John a good or bad king?' The purpose of this assessment is to evaluate the pupils' understanding of sources and their different interpretations (incorporating Key Elements 3a, 3b, 4a and 4b). The teaching and the assessment was spread over three lessons – a preparatory lesson, the completion of a set of questions and finally the assessment lesson. This skill area would be revisited as an assessment in Years 8 and 9, using different historical topics, but providing the opportunity for pupils to see progression in their own learning. A test took the form of open-ended questions, which required the pupils to write extended answers; thus differentiation was by outcome. Prior to the test, the pupils had been taught a variety of important concepts that had been built into the department's unit of work on King John. These included activities that encouraged the pupils to assess the usefulness of different sources on the king and consider why people had different opinions about him. These activities were essential in establishing, at the very least, a basic understanding of source interpretation; the very skills being assessed at the end of the unit.

On the day of the test, the pupils were each given a copy of the mark scheme, which takes the form of a pupil-speak 'success ladder'. The success criteria were explained to them, highlighting examples of progression on the ladder. They were encouraged to use this mark scheme as a checklist of things to do during the test in order to achieve the level they were targeting. The class was then given a collection of sources on King John, a question sheet and asked to complete the assessment.

WWW   The sources and comments about their authors, the 'success ladder' together with the questions set for the pupils and peer assessment sheets may be seen at

http://www.routledge.com/textbooks/9780415370240

Peer assessment lesson

The lesson outlined was one-hour long and was delivered to a mixed ability Year 7 group. In pairs, the pupils were given a set of statements taken from the mark scheme and asked to put them in order according to their difficulty. This starter activity provided the class with an opportunity to understand both the learning objectives of the lesson and the progression of skills within the success ladder.

The learning objectives were reinforced on the board and the pupils were given back their completed assessment answers and question materials. They were then asked to swap their answer sheet and success ladder sheet with their partner. The pupils were asked to read through their partner's answers and, using the success ladder, work their way up it, ensuring that their peer had met all the criteria for each level. Pupils were encouraged to highlight where their partner had demonstrated a particular skill in their answers; a highlighter pen and comment in the margin enabled students to share evidence of progress with their partner later in the lesson. This process ended when the marker had reached a place on the ladder where it was felt the partner could go no further, thus establishing the level their answer deserved.

The most important part of this lesson centred on the discussion that now took place between each pair of pupils. Focusing on one set of assessment answers at a time, the peer marker fed back the decisions they had made about the work in front of them, making reference to both the success ladder and the highlighted evidence in the answers. The pupil being assessed then had the opportunity to either agree with their peer marker or seek further evidence within their answers that might put them in a different place on the success ladder. Only by working with the peer marker and only if in joint agreement, could the original level awarded be amended.

The final activity of the lesson was the completion by the peer marker of the 'peer level and comment' boxes on the success ladder sheet. This really does provide evidence for the teacher of just how well the students have understood the success criteria of the assessment. An example of these peer comment boxes completed is flagged up on the board and explained by the teacher, outlining how the peer marker should decide on what is to be written on the success ladder sheet. The recording of a level, followed by a positive comment about their peer's work was straightforward enough, but several peer markers in the group needed further assurance as to what they should write in the final and most important two peer comment boxes on the sheet. The construction of a positive peer comment from the mark scheme should come from the set of statements describing the level the peer has been awarded. Logically, it is one of those statements that the peer marker has already confirmed they have fulfilled and should be recorded in a positive manner on the sheet. Using similar logic, it is from the set of statements describing the level above the one the pupil has been awarded, from which a realistic and achievable target should be taken.

As a plenary, two pairs of pupils were selected to share with the rest of the group their experiences of peer marking, talking through the comments they had made about their partner's work and justifying the level they had awarded their work. Care was taken to select pairs able to articulate the process with prompting from the teacher. From this feedback to the rest of the group, the teacher is able to relate this discussion to what has been achieved by everyone in the classroom, who could now see that the lesson's learning outcomes had been met.

An analysis of pupil responses to the lesson

All the pupils in this lesson not only completed written peer comments and targets, but were also asked to feed back their own ideas regarding the aspects of the lesson they felt went well, and any difficulties they experienced during the peer assessment process. Some clear patterns did emerge from this feedback:

- All pupils understood where their targets had come from on the mark scheme and how this would lead to their progression in this skill when revisited in a future assessment.

- Many of the pupils benefited from marking their peers' work as it gave them the opportunity to see a different level of answer to their own. Less able pupils, in particular, had begun to identify what their more able peers had included in their work to achieve a high level, giving them a clearer understanding of what was missing from their own responses.

- A number of pupils commented on how it was easier to understand what they had done well, and what needed to be done next time to improve, when it was explained to them by their peers. Physically being shown by their peers the relevant evidence of success in their work reinforced this understanding.

- A minority of less able pupils still found understanding some of the more challenging historical concepts difficult. The question of why sources can be viewed in different ways proved beyond some students, who still relied on the misconception that 'every source is fact' as a basis for their answers.

Issues arising from these lessons

1   The lessons showed that the use of peer assessment has *a positive effect on the less able pupils*. This is consistent with the work of Black and Wiliam (1998) in promoting such forms of formative assessment. The process can give a great impetus to their self-improvement as they gain a clearer idea of what they have achieved and of what is needed. In this they benefit from the statements of progress rather than grades or marks. The nature of the pairings needs thought. The King John lessons suggest the value of pairing pupils of differing abilities but not excessively so. This enables the teacher to give the pair a success ladder appropriate to their ability. There is case for giving different parts of the ladder to different pairs.

2   Using peer assessment illustrates yet again *the value of pupil talk* in the classroom if purposely employed. Dialogue takes place with pupils using their own language and at the same time giving meaning in their own terms to the language of the mark scheme (Activity 10.4). Working with each other they are likely to be less inhibited than in teacher–pupil exchanges.

3   Peer assessment can take more time than that usually allotted to a topic. In this example the study of King John can stretch over three or four lessons. However, it may be

---

Activity 10.4   The value of discussion in peer assessment

Select a couple of pairs of pupils to go through the procedure of peer assessment using a particular written exercise that you have devised with a 'success ladder' mark scheme. Using a tape recorder, record the discussions that take place between the pupils as they provide feedback. Then consider the following questions:

1   Do the pupils use the language in the mark scheme accurately when providing feedback? (This provides you with an indication of how well the pupils understand the statements on the mark scheme.)

2   Do the pupils refer to their peer's work when providing evidence of what has been achieved in accordance with the mark scheme? (A pupil needs to understand how a statement from the mark scheme has been successfully met by what has been written down by their peer.)

claimed that this is time well spent if the learning through the assessment process really does advance pupils' understanding of a particular concept as well as reinforcing their knowledge. In *Good Assessment Practice in History* (Ofsted 2003), HMI who welcomed classroom teaching where 'sufficient time is given in lessons for discussion of assessment criteria or outcomes, which is valuable in focusing pupils' attention on what they need to do next or how to improve.'

4   It is important to stress the need to have *limited expectations* from your early efforts. As in many features of your developing competence as a history teacher it is important to keep analysing what you are doing but not to be too self-critical. What is being attempted here is quite sophisticated and success will only develop over time. The pupils themselves need to be able to adjust to the use of self-assessment. Success depends on the pupils understanding the 'success criteria', which means you have to work hard at the language used as some pupils will find this difficult. One of the most important parts of formative assessment is how you use the information from peer assessment to adjust your future teaching so seek further opportunities for using peer assessment.

5   The 'success ladder' used in the mark scheme was very much a compromise between the National Curriculum levels and the historical topic. It is far from ideal but operates within the current assessment climate in schools. Nevertheless it is important that you think about the wider issues and try to *experiment with creating your own mark schemes*, schemes, which are content and concept specific (Burnham and Brown, 2004). This pushes you to be able to articulate very clearly and precisely what your objectives are and how you see progress in that particular topic, skill or concept.

Activity 10.5 will encourage you to think about the criteria you would use in assessing pupils' work. The basic questions are 'What makes this piece of work better than that one?' and 'To what extent does this pupil show an understanding of the knowledge, skills and concepts I am trying to assess?' To use peer assessment successfully you need to be able to express such understanding in words your pupils will be able to understand when they are attempting an exercise or assessing the work of a peer.

Activity 10.5   Devising your own 'success ladder' mark scheme

Using the example of the King John material, try to devise your own 'success ladder' mark scheme for a piece of written work your pupils will be doing. Consider the following points:

1   The ladder does not have to make use of the National Curriculum Levels. In your first efforts keep it simple, using the proforma below, e.g. What do I want from a piece of work that I would assess as excellent; then very good, good, satisfactory?

2   Consider what marking criteria you had in mind for this piece of work and how it might be broken down into specific skills (e.g. explaining causes, linking causes together and explaining why one cause is more important than another). You will probably find it helpful to adapt the relevant parts of Tim Lomas (1990), *Teaching and Assessing Historical Understanding*, London, Historical Association, and Martin Hunt (1997) *Thinking It Through*, to be found on http://www.uea.ac.uk/~m242/historypgce/planning.

3   Consider how some students will show different levels of success in demonstrating the skills you are assessing; try to make sure your 'success ladder' indicates the progression that will be made across the ability range.

Activity 10.5 *continued*

4   Share these success criteria with your students before they attempt the written task you have set them. Make sure they understand the terms you have used in your mark scheme.

5   As your students become familiar with the mark schemes, repeat this process of planning a mark scheme, but involve the students in agreeing the mark scheme with you, giving them joint ownership of what is being assessed.

Title of Work:			
Excellent	a)		Teacher Comment:
	b)		
	c)		
	d)		
Very Good	a)		Peer General Comment:
	b)		
	c)		
	d)		
Good	a)		Peer Comment from Mark Scheme:
	b)		
	c)		
	d)		
Satisfactory	a)		Peer Target from Mark Scheme:
	b)		
	c)		
	d)		
Target One:			
Target Two:			

SUMMARY

Peer assessment is the first step on a ladder that ultimately leads to students becoming reflective and independent learners. If we can give students the opportunity to understand clearly what it is they need to do to reach a particular level of attainment in history, progression in our subject will almost always be guaranteed. Giving students ownership of their peers' feedback and target setting, illustrates to them what progress they themselves have made and focuses them on what will become their own meaningful and achievable targets for next time. Peer assessment is thus one very practical form of assessment for learning although of course not exclusively so. You will always be looking for opportunities as they occur to develop pupils' understanding of what it means 'to get better' in history.

FURTHER READING

Assessment Reform Group (1999) *Assessment for Learning: Beyond the Black Box*, Cambridge: University of Cambridge, Faculty of Education.

Black, P., Harrison, C., Lee, C., Marshall, B. and Wiliam, D. (2002) *Working Inside the Black Box: Assessment for Learning in the Classroom*, London: King's College.

Black, P. and Wiliam, D. (1998) *Inside the Black Box: Raising Standards through Classroom Assessment*, London: King's College.

Burnham, S. and Brown, G. (2004) 'Assessment without levels', *Teaching History*, 115.

DfES (2004) *Assessment for Learning: Whole School Training Materials*, London: DfES Publications.

Cottingham, M. (2004) 'Dr Black Box *or* How I learned to stop worrying and love assessment', *Teaching History*, 115.

Bibliography

Assessment Reform Group (1999) *Assessment for Learning: Beyond the Black Box*, Cambridge: University of Cambridge, Faculty of Education.

Banham, D. and Dawson, I. (2002) 'Thinking from the inside: je suis le roi', *Teaching History*, 108.

Biddulph, M. and Adey, K. (2003) 'Perceptions v reality: students' experiences of learning history and geography at Key Stage 4', *The Curriculum Journal*, 14 (3).

Black, P., Harrison, C., Lee, C., Marshall, B. and Wiliam, D. (2002) *Working Inside the Black Box: Assessment for Learning in the Classroom*, London: King's College.

Black, P. and Wiliam, D. (1998) *Inside the Black Box: Raising Standards through Classroom Assessment*, London: King's College.

Brien, T. (2001) *Enabling Inclusion*, Norwich: The Stationery Office.

Burnham, S. and Brown, G. (2004) 'Assessment without levels', *Teaching History*, 115.

Byrom, J. (1999) *Minds and Machines, Britain 1750–1900*, London, Longman.

Byrom, J. (2003) 'Continuity and progression', in *Past Forward: A Vision of School History, 2002–2012*, London: Historical Association.

Byrom, J., Counsell, C., Riley, M. and Stephens-Wood, P. (1997) *Changing Minds*, Harlow: Longman.

Card, J. (2004) 'Seeing double: how one period visualizes another', *Teaching History*, 117.

Carr, E. H. (1961) *What Is History?*, London: Macmillan.

Chapman, A. (2003) 'Camels, diamonds and counterfactuals: a model for teaching causal reasoning', *Teaching History*, 112.

Clare, J. D. (1997) *A United Kingdom 1500–1750*, Walton-on Thames: Nelson.

Clark, V. (2001) 'Illuminating the shadow; making progress happen in causal thinking through speaking and listening', *Teaching History*, 105.

Cottingham, M. (2004) 'Dr Black Box *or* How I learned to stop worrying and love assessment', *Teaching History*, 115.

Counsell, C. (1997) *Analytical and Discursive Writing at KS3*, London: Historical Association.

Counsell, C. (2004) 'Looking through a Josephine Butler-shaped window: focussing pupils' thinking on historical significance', *Teaching History*, 114.

Croft, M. (2005) 'The Tudor monarchy in crisis: using a historian's account to stretch the most able students in Year 8', *Teaching History*, 119.

Cunnah, W. (2000) 'History teaching, literacy and special educational needs', in J. Arthur and R. Phillips (eds) *Issues in History Teaching*, London: Routledge.

Davies, I. and Williams, R. (1998) 'Interpretations of history'. Issues for teachers in the development of pupils' understanding', *Teaching History*, 91.

Davies, P., Lynch, D. and Davis, R. (2003) *Enlivening Secondary History: 40 Classroom Activities for Teachers and Pupils*, London: Routledge.

DfES (2001) *Numeracy Across the Curriculum*, www.standards.dfes.gov.uk/keystage3/resput/num_xc_webresources

DfES (2004) *Assessment for Learning: Whole School Training Materials*, London: DfES.

Evans, R. J. (1997) *In Defence of History*, London: Granta Books.

Fisher, P. (ed.) (2002) *Thinking through History*, Cambridge: Chris Kingston Publishing.

Grosvenor, I. (2000) 'History and the perils of multiculturalism in 1990s Britain', in J. Arthur and R. Phillips (eds) *Issues in Teaching History*, London: Routledge.

Hammond, K. (1999) 'And Joe arrives . . .: stretching the very able pupil in the mixed ability classroom', *Teaching History*, 94.

Harris, R. (2005) 'Does differentiation have to mean different?', *Teaching History*, ???

Harris, R. and Luff, I. (2004) *Meeting Special Needs in the Curriculum: History*, London: David Fulton Publishers.

Haydn, T., Arthur, J. and Hunt, M. (2001) *Learning to Teach History in the Secondary School*, 2nd edn, London: Routledge.

Haydn, T. (2000) 'Information and communications technology in the history classroom', in J. Arthur and R. Phillips (eds) *Issues in History Teaching*, London: Routledge.

Haydn, T. and Counsell, C. (eds) (2003) *History, ICT and Learning in the Secondary School*, London: Routledge.

Historical Association (2005) *History 14–19 Report and Recommendations to the Secretary of State*, London: History Association.

Hunt, M. (2000) 'Teaching historical significance', in J. Arthur and R. Phillips (eds) *Issues in History Teaching*, London: Routledge, pp. 39–53.

Husbands, C. (1996) *What Is History Teaching? Language, Ideas and Meaning in Learning about the Past*, Buckingham: Open University Press.

Lee, P. (1998) '"A lot of guess work goes on"': children's understanding of historical accounts', *Teaching History*, 92.

Lee, P., Ashby, R. and Dickinson, A. (1995) 'Progression in children's ideas about history', in M. Booth (ed.) *Progression in Learning*, Clevedon: Multilingual Matters Ltd.

Lee, P. and Shemilt, D. (2003) 'A scaffold not a cage: progression and progression models in history', *Teaching History*, 113.

Lee, P. and Shemilt, D. (2004) 'Progression in understanding about historical accounts', *Teaching History*, 117.

Lewis, M. and Wray, D. (1994) *Working with Writing Frames: Developing Children's Non-Fiction Writing*, London: Scholastic.

Lomas, T. (1990) *Teaching and Assessing Historical Understanding*, London: Historical Association.

Luff, I. (2000) 'I've been in the Reichstag: rethinking role play', *Teaching History*, 100.

Luff, I. (2003) 'Stretching the strait jacket of assessment: use of role play and practical demonstration to enrich pupil experience of history at GCSE and beyond', *Teaching History*, 113.

McAleavy, T. (2000) 'Teaching about interpretations', in J. Arthur and R. Philips (eds) *Issues in Teaching History*, London: Routledge.

McCully, A. (1997) 'Key questions, planning and extended writing', *Teaching History*, 89, 31–55.

Ofsted (2001) *History in the Secondary School*, e-publication.

Ofsted (2002) *Good Assessment Practice in History*, London: The Stationery Office.

Phillips, I. (2002) 'History: Mathematics or History with Mathematics: does it add up?', *Teaching History*, 107.

Phillips, R. (2001) 'Initial stimulus material', *Teaching History*, 105.

Reed, L. (2001) *Child Labor and the British Industrial Revolution*, Mackinac Center of Public Policy.

Scott, J. (1990) *Understanding Cause and Effect*, Harlow: Longman.

Shephard, C. and Moore, A. (2005) *The Making of the UK Teachers' Resource Book*, London: John Murray.

Smith, P. (2001) 'Mick didn't like the sound of quitting . . .', *Teaching History*, 103.

Smith, P. (2002) 'International relations at GCSE – they just can't get enough of it', *Teaching History*, 108.

Snelson, H., Mawson, K. and Justice, S. (2002) 'Getting the whole school buzzing about history: The South Hunsley Story', *Teaching History*, 108.

Steele, I. (1976) *Developments in History Teaching*, Open Books.

Thompson, E. P. (1980) *The Making of the English Working Class*, London: Penguin.

Walsh, B. (2005) *Exciting ICT in History*, Network Educational Press.

Wrenn, A. (1999) 'Substantial sculptures or sad little plaques? Making interpretations matter to Year 9', *Teaching History*, 97.

Wrenn, A. (2002) 'Equines: voices of silent slaves', *Teaching History*, 107.

Index

Liverpool Hope
University

This item is to be returned on or before the last
due date stamped below .

Items can be renewed 3 times unseen.If a fourth
renewal is required the item must be brought
to the library.

Liverpool Hope University
The Sheppard-Worlock Library
Tel: 0151 291 2000
http://www.hope.ac.uk/library